PRIESTCRAFT
AND THE
SLAUGHTERHOUSE RELIGIO

Other books by the author:

The War System and You

My Country - Right Or Wrong?

The Power Within

PRIESTCRAFT
AND THE
SLAUGHTERHOUSE RELIGION

° A rejoinder to the notion that the United States
  was designed to promote the Christian religion.

° A perspective on current fundamentalism.

° A plea for a governed world.

Edited and Commentaries by:

Jack Lasley

NISGO Publications
Post Office Box 549
Cocoa, Florida 32923

TO THE READER

The radical fundamentalists would like for you to surrender your powers to think critically and to reason for yourself. Some of their institutional churches would seek to make of you a shorn sheep, babbling in public as "evidence" that you have been filled "with the Holy Ghost." Such a public display of mental vapidness is the ultimate degradation - conceived by the radical church - to reduce its members to the servile, unreasoning, pliable, sniveling supplicants required for the infilling of its theology and political ideas. The church loves to see such concomitants of servility. These shepherds are not content to shear away the sins of their sheep, but are content only with thought control. Yet what the world and the church both need is not more sheep shorn of their reason but more responsible, reasoning individuals.

Our nation's Founding Fathers were well aware of the Inquisition and other religious excesses, both here and abroad, that denied individual freedom. They believed in the use of government to bring together diverse individuals and political entities into a union of the whole to protect individual rights and freedoms. If we come to share their faith in representative government, world peace can be achieved.

Today the same type of thinking that brought about the Inquisition and other forms of religious intolerance in the days of the Founding Fathers, is at work again. But this time it comes from a different direction: the leadership of the radical fundamentalist right.

The principal danger from radical fundamentalism is that through the use of thought control, superstition, myth, and prejudice, it will block the use of government from its highest and best use: That of bringing the blessing of peace with justice to each of us.

Jack Lasley

Dedicated . . .

to all people who have not surrendered
their God given right to reason for themselves.

Acknowledgment . . .

the invaluable assistance of
Jacqueline M. Kinsley is deeply appreciated.

CONTENTS

Preface

Fear and guilt are the stock in trade of the radical Christian fundamentalist.

This book is a plea not to let these factors keep us from taking those steps necessary to rid the world of the threat of nuclear annihilation.

J.L.

THE

WAY

IT

WAS

The United States
Was Not Created To Be
A Christian Nation

Suppose you were to travel to Washington, D.C. in search of evidence that the United States was a Christian nation. You would find the cornerstone of our capital building, laid by George Washington, has had added to it words of Daniel Webster referring to God. "In God We Trust" is on some of our money and emblazoned on the speaker's chair in the House of Representatives. Journey over to the Supreme Court building and hear the crier open court with the words: "God save the United States." Over at the White House there is an inscription asking the blessings of heaven on its occupants. At the very pinacle of the highest edifice is etched the words: "Praise Be to God," and within the Washington Monument are several quotations from the Bible.

Go into the Library of Congress and you will see a number of Bible verses on the walls. In the National Archives building you will find "Nature's God" is mentioned in the Declaration of Independence, and "the year of our Lord" in the Constitution. Congress is opened with prayer; oaths of office, and the oath administered before taking testimony in court, mention the name of God. There was even a decision of the Supreme Court in 1892, while not deciding the matter, stating we are a Christian nation.

As if this is not enough, your pastor likely tells you our nation was founded to propagate the Christian religion. What, then, are you to say? Surely with such evidence you must conclude this nation was designed to be a Christian nation.

Well, don't stop now. Keep digging. What about all those explorers and settlers kneeling in the sand after they landed? Clearly they were Christian bent on establishing a Christian nation. One's mind naturally pictures Columbus, the Santa Maria, El Salvadore. Think too of those at Jamestown in 1606 who spoke of "propagating the Christian religion." Their first recorded act was to erect a cross and worship. Then don't forget the Mayflower Compact when, in 1620 at Plymouth, some of our stalwart forefathers wrote that they undertook their mission for the "advancement of the Christian faith." And there is the Connecticut constitution of 1639 which says those who settled there came to "maintain and preserve the Gospel of Jesus Christ"; and, there is the First Pennsylvania Charter of Privileges which makes reference to Jesus Christ as the "savior of the world."

So. . . with such overwhelming evidence, you must be convinced by now that this nation was founded by Christians, for Christians, and for the propagation of Christianity. Well. . . don't you believe it!

What has been left out of this piece - to this point - are the actions of Christians between the middle sixteen hundreds and the time the Constitution was drawn.

The mental pictures of Pilgrims at Thanksgiving; or, of an explorer wading ashore, thrusting a cross-decorated flag in the sand, whipping out his sword, and kneeling in prayer - represent only part of the story. It was the period **after** the Christians landed that caused the Founding Fathers concern as to the course of religious freedom in our new nation.

What about those witch-burnings in Salem? Yes, and there were other excesses. In Virginia the Church of England was established as the state church. Laws were passed prescribing horrendous punishments for those who did not toady to the religious mark.

Early settlers in Virginia continued the traditions of the Anglican Church and were intolerant of other faiths; discrimination abounded for over 100 years. Preachers had to be licensed by the state. Citizens were fined and imprisoned for failure to support church doctrine; and, in New England, scripture had been used by Calvinists in power to ban a wide variety of activities.

In the critical post-Revolutionary period, we had in our country Baptists, Presbyterians, Quakers, Mennonites, Jews, Roman Catholics, Anabaptists, French Huguenots, Dunkers, Jesuits, Waldenes, and others - a flock of denominations and creeds.

While the Founding Fathers generally resisted the biblical view of creation and attempts to legislate acceptance of ecclesiastical teachings dealing with the universe and man's role in it, their own personal creeds ranged from the Puritanism of Samuel Adams to the Deism of Paine and others. Among them it was God, yes; Jesus, yes, no, and maybe.

Jefferson in particular was concerned that religious beliefs not be entangled with government sponsorship or endorsement. The idea of enforced religion was another of his concerns. Religion was an intensely personal matter for him and those associated with him in nation-building. Ironically the religious persecutions the settlers had fled Europe to escape had been transplanted by them in the New World. So the Constitutional Convention was concerned with religious abuses that had taken place here as well as in Europe.

In Europe Anabaptists had been burned at the stake. Quakers and Jews persecuted and killed. Tyndale had been both strangled and burned for publishing a translation of the Bible, as were some of those who dared distribute it. Puritans had been imprisoned.

In our new land, Quakers had been burned in Massachusetts. By law all "opposers of the worship of God" were declared not to be free men. This came from the very Puritans that had been persecuted themselves in Europe.

In Virginia, Baptists, Quakers, and Catholics were made unwelcome. Bail was not granted, and even the publication of Quaker beliefs brought a jail sentence. In Pennsylvania all citizens were required by law to attend church or prove they had been reading the Bible during church services.

Catholics who had found freedom in Maryland, soon lost it when Protestants came to power.

It was evident to those who gathered in Philadelphia to frame our Constitution that complete forbearance by government from the business of religion was to be sought. A man's religion was between himself and his God. It was not government business.

Clearly the Founding Fathers believed in God. Most would even consider themselves Christian, but their brand of Christianity was not of the so-called "full gospel, charismatic, evangelical," fundamentalist variety; examples: Franklin edited the Lord's Prayer, and Jefferson re-wrote the New Testament. Some questioned the validity of biblical miracles, and even the historicity of the life of Jesus. What these young men sought was a new nation wherein there would be no government intrusion into the religious lives of the citizenry.

At the particular insistence of Jefferson and Madison, they wrote into the First Amendment: "Congress shall make no law respecting an establishment of religion, or prohibiting the free exercise thereof. . . ." The term "establishment of religion" is not resonant to the modern ear. We do not now use the word "establishment" as they did. A true feeling for what they meant by this word and the purpose behind the insertion of the First Amendment into our Constitution can be gained by understanding the religious views of its key framers and those who set the tone for this cornerstone of our religious freedom.

Now let us proceed to hear what a representative group had to say.[1]

[THOMAS JEFFERSON: Author of the Declaration of Independence; third President of the United States; father of the University of Virginia.]

Subject & Comment: **Jesus Christ Only, Rejected**

Jefferson: I proposed the demolition of the church establishment, and the freedom of religion. It could only be done by degrees; to wit, the Act of 1776, c. 2 exempted dissenters from contributions to the Church, and left the Church clergy to be supported by voluntary contributions of their own sect; was continued from year to year, and made perpetual 1779, c 36. I prepared the act for religious freedom in 1779, as part of the revisal, which was not reported to the Assembly till 1779, and that

[1] Arranged according to continuity of subject matter.

particular law not passed till 1785, and then by the efforts of Mr. Madison.

* * *

The bill for establishing religious freedom, the principles of which had, to a certain degree, been enacted before, I had drawn in all the latitude of reason and right. It still met with opposition; but, with some mutilations in the preamble, it was finally passed; and a singular proposition proved that its protection of opinion was meant to be universal. Where the preamble declares, that coercion is a departure from the plan of the holy author of our religion, an amendment was proposed, by inserting the word "Jesus Christ" so that it should read, "a departure from the plan of Jesus Christ, the holy author of our religion"; the insertion was rejected by a great majority, in proof that they meant to comprehend, within the mantle of its protection, the Jew and the Gentile, the Christian and the Mohometan, the Hindoo, and the Infidel of every denomination.[2]

Subject and Comment: **Human Mind Freed From Vassalage**

Jefferson: The Virginia act for religious freedom has been received with infinite approbation in Europe, and propagated with enthusiasm. I do not mean by the governments, but by the individuals who compose them. It has been translated into French and Italian, has been sent to most of the courts of Europe, and has been the best evidence of the falsehood of those reports which stated us to be in anarchy. It is inserted in the new Encyclopedie, and is appearing in most of the publications respecting America. In fact, it is comfortable to see the standard of reason at length erected after so many ages, during which the human mind has been held in vassalage by kings, priests, and nobles; and it is honorable for us, to have produced the first legislature who had the courage to declare,

[2] From Jefferson's autobiography. See: Norman Cousins, **In God We Trust** (Harper & Brothers, New York, 1958), p. 120.

that the reason of man may be trusted with the formation of his own opinions.[3]

Subject and Comment: **We Persecuted Our Own People**

Jefferson: The first settlers in this country were emigrants from England, of the English church, just at a point of time when it was flushed with complete victory over the religions of all other persuasions. Possessed, as they became, of the powers of making, administering, and executing the laws, they showed equal intolerance in this country with their Presbyterian brethren, who had emigrated to the northern government. The poor Quakers were flying from persecution in England. They cast their eyes on these new countries as asylums of civil and religious freedom; but they found them free only for the reigning sect. Several acts of the Virginia Assembly of 1659, 1662, and 1693, had made it penal in parents to refuse to have their children baptized; had prohibited the unlawful assembling of Quakers; had made it penal for any master of a vessel to bring a Quaker into the state; had ordered those already here, and such as should come hereafter to be imprisoned until they should abjure the country; provided a milder punishment for their first and second return, but death for their third; had inhibited all persons from suffering their meeting in or near their houses, entertaining them individually, or disposing of books which supported their tenets.

If no executions took place here, as did in New England, it was not owing to the moderation of the church, or spirit of the legislature, as may be inferred from the law itself; but to historical circumstances which have not been handed down to us. The Anglicans retained full possession of the country about a century. Other opinions began then to creep in, and the great care of the government to support their own church, having begotten an equal degree of indolence in its clergy, two-thirds of the people had become dissenters

[3] Letter to James Madison, December 16, 1786.

at the commencement of the present revolution. The laws, indeed, were still oppressive on them, but the spirit of the one party had subsided into moderation, and the other had risen to a degree of determination which commanded respect.

The present state of our laws on the subject of religion is this. The Convention of May, 1776, in their declaration of rights, declared it to be a truth, and a natural right, that the exercise of religion should be free; but when they proceeded to form on that declaration the ordinance of government, instead of taking up every principle declared in the bill of rights, and guarding it by legislative sanction, they passed over that which asserted our religious rights, leaving them as they found them. The same convention, however, when they met as a member of the general assembly in October, 1776, repealed all acts of Parliament which had rendered criminal the maintaining any opinions in matters of religion, the fore bearing to repair to church, and the exercising any mode of worship; and suspended the laws giving salaries to the clergy, which suspension was made perpetual in October, 1779. Statutory oppression in religion being thus wiped away, we remain at present under those only imposed by the common law, or by our own acts of assembly. At the common law, heresy was a capital offense, punishable by burning. Its definition was left to the ecclesiastical judges, before whom the conviction was, till the statute of I.El.c.I. circumscribed it, by declaring, that nothing should be deemed heresy, but what had been so determined by authority of the canonical scriptures, or by one of the four first general councils, or by other council having for the grounds of their declaration the express and plain words of the scriptures. Heresy, thus circumscribed, being an offense at the common law, our act of assembly of October 1776, c. 17, gives cognizance of it to the general court, by declaring that the jurisdiction of that court shall be general in all matters at the common law. The execution is by writ De hoeretico comburendo [On the burning of a heretic]. By our own act of assembly of 1705, c. 30. if a person brought up in the Christian religion denies the being of a God, or the Trinity, or asserts there are more gods than one, or denies the Christian religion to be true, or the scriptures to be of divine authority, he is punishable on the first offense by incapacity to hold any office or employment ecclesiastical, civil or military; on the second by disability to sue, to take any gift or legacy, to be guardian, executor, or administrator, and by three years' imprisonment without bail. A father's right to the custody of his own children being founded in law on his right of guardianship, this being taken away, they may of course be severed from him, and put by the authority of the court into more orthodox hands.

This is a summary view of that religious slavery, under which a people have been willing to remain, who have lavished their lives and fortunes for the establishment of their civil freedom. The error seems not sufficiently eradicated, that the operations of the mind, as well as the acts of the body, are subject to the coercion of the laws. But our rulers can have no authority over such natural rights, only as we have submitted to them. The rights of conscience we never submitted, we could not submit. We are answerable for them to our God. The legitimate powers of government extend to such acts only as are injurious to others. But it does me no injury for my neighbor to say there are twenty Gods, or no God. It neither picks my pocket nor breaks my leg. If it be said, his testimony in a court of justice cannot be relied on, reject it then, and be the stigma on him. Constraint may make him worse by making him a hypocrite, but it will never make him a truer man. It may fix him obstinately in his errors, but will not cure them.

Reason and free inquiry are the only effectual agents against terror. Give a loose to them, they will support true religion, by bringing every false one to their tribunal, to the test of their investigation. They are the natural enemies of error, and of error only. Had not the Roman government permitted free inquiry, Christianity could never have been introduced. Had not free inquiry been indulged at the era of reformation, the corruptions of Christianity could not have been purged away. If it be restrained now, the present corruptions will be protected and new ones encouraged. Was the government to prescribe to us our medicine and diet, our bodies would be in such keeping as our souls are now. Thus in France the emetic was once forbidden as a medicine, and the potatoe as an article of food.

Government is just as infallible, too, when it fixes systems in physics. Galileo was sent to the inquisition for affirming that the earth was a sphere; the government had declared it to be as flat as a trencher, and Galileo was obliged to abjure his error. This error at length prevailed, the earth became a globe, and Descartes declared it was whirled around its axis by a vortex. The government in which he lived was wise enough to see that this was no question of civil jurisdiction, or we should all have been involved by authority in vortices. In fact, the vortices have been exploded, and the Newtonian principle of gravitation is now more firmly established, on the basis of reason, than it would be were the government to step in, and make it an article of necessary faith. Reason and experiment have been indulged, and error has fled before them. It is error alone which needs the support of government. Truth can stand by itself.

Subject opinion to coercion: whom will you make your inquisitors? Fallible men; men governed by bad passions, by private as well as public reasons. And why subject it to coercion? To produce uniformity. But is uniformity of opinion desirable? No more than of face and stature. Introduce the bed of Procrustes then, and as there is danger that the large men may beat the small, make us all of a size, by lopping the former and stretching the latter.

Difference of opinion is advantageous in religion. The several sects perform the office of a censor morum over such other. Is uniformity attainable? Millions of innocent men, women, and children, since

12 /

the introduction of Christianity, have been burnt,
tortured, fined, imprisoned; yet we have not advanced
one inch toward uniformity. What has been the
effect of coercion? To make one half the world
fools and the other half hypocrites. To support
roguery and error all over the earth. Let us reflect
that it is inhabited by a thousand millions of people.
That these profess probably a thousand different
systems of religion. That ours is but one of that
thousand. That if there be but one right, and ours
that one, we should wish to see the nine hundred
and ninety-nine wandering sects gathered into the
fold of truth. But against such a majority we cannot
effect this by force. Reason and persuasion are
the only practicable instruments. To make way
for these, free inquiry must be indulged; how can
we wish others to indulge it while we refuse it
ourselves. But every state, says an inquisitor, has
established some religion. No two, say I, have
established the same. Is this a proof of the
infallibility of establishments? Our sister states
of Pennsylvania and New York, however, have long
subsisted without any establishment at all. The
experiment was new and doubtful when they made
it. It has answered beyond conception. They flourish
infinitely. Religion is well supported; of various
kinds, indeed, but all good enough; all sufficient
to preserve peace and order; or if a sect arises,
whose tenets would subvert morals, good sense has
fair play, and reasons and laughs it out of doors,
without suffering the state to be troubled with
it. They do not hang more malefactors than we
do. They are not more disturbed with religious
dissensions than we are. On the contrary, their
harmony is unparalleled, and can be ascribed to
nothing but their unbounded tolerance, because there
is no other circumstance in which they differ from
every nation on earth. They have made the happy
discovery, that the way to silence religious disputes,
is to take no notice of them.

Let us too give this experiment fair play, and
get rid, while we may, of those tyrannical laws.
It is true, we are as yet secured against them by

the spirit of the times. I doubt whether the people of this country would suffer an execution for heresy, or a three years imprisonment for not comprehending the mysteries of the Trinity. But is the spirit of the people an infallible, a permanent reliance? Is it government? Is this the kind of protection we receive in return for the rights we give up? Besides, the spirit of the times may alter, will alter. Our rulers will become corrupt, our people careless. A single zealot may commence persecutor, and better men be his victims.

It can never be too often repeated, that the time for fixing every essential right on a legal basis is while our rulers are honest, and ourselves united. From the conclusion of this war we shall be going down hill. It will not then be necessary to resort every moment to the people for support. They will be forgotten, therefore, and their rights disregarded. They will forget themselves, but in the sole faculty of making money, and will never think of uniting to effect a due respect for their rights. The shackles, therefore, which shall not be knocked off at the conclusion of this war, will remain on us long, will be made heavier and heavier till our rights shall revive or expire in a convulsion.[4]

Subject and Comment: **Tax Moneys for School Prayer?**

Jefferson: That to compel a man to furnish contributions of money for the propagation of opinions which he disbelieves, is sinful and tyrannical; that even the forcing of him to support this or that teacher of his own religious persuasion, is depriving him of the comfortable liberty of giving his contributions to the particular pastor whose morals he would make his pattern, and whose powers he feels most persuasive to righteousness, and is withdrawing from the ministry those temporal rewards, which, proceeding from an approbation of their personal conduct, are an additional incitement to earnest and unremitting labors for the instruction of mankind; that our civil rights have no dependence on our religious opinions more

[4] From Jefferson's notes on the Religious Freedom Act of 1786.

than on our opinions in physics or geometry;

that therefore the proscribing any citizen as unworthy the public confidence by laying upon him an incapacity of being called to offices of trust and emolument, unless he profess or renounce this or that religious opinion, is depriving him injuriously of those privileges and advantages to which in common with his fellow citizens he has a natural right;

that it tends also to corrupt the principles of that very religion it is meant to encourage, by bribing, with a monopoly of worldly honors and emoluments, those who will externally profess and conform to it;

that though indeed these are criminal who do not withstand such temptation, yet neither are those innocent who lay the bait in their way;

that to suffer the civil magistrate to intrude his powers into the field of opinion, and to restrain the profession or propagation of principles, on supposition of their ill tendency, is a dangerous fallacy, which at once destroys all religious liberty, because he being of course judge of that tendency, will make his opinions the rule of judgment, and approve or condemn the sentiments of others only as they shall square with or differ from his own;

that it is time enough for the rightful purposes of civil government for its officers to interfere when principles break out into overt acts against peace and good order;

and finally, that truth is great and will prevail if left to herself, that she is the proper and sufficient antagonist to error, and has nothing to fear from the conflict, unless by human interposition disarmed of her natural weapons, free argument and debate, errors ceasing to be dangerous when it is permitted freely to contradict them;

Be it therefore enacted by the General Assembly, That no man shall be compelled to frequent or support any religious worship, place or ministry whatsoever, nor shall be enforced, restrained, molested, or burthened in his body or goods, nor shall otherwise suffer on account of his religious opinions or belief; but that all men shall be free to profess and by argument to maintain their opinions in matters of religion, and that the same shall in no wise diminish, enlarge, or effect their civil capacities.

And though we well know that this assembly, elected by the people for the ordinary purposes of legislation only, have no power to restrain the acts of succeeding assemblies, constituted with powers equal to our own, and that therefore to declare this act irrevocable, would be of no effect in law, yet we are free to declare, and do declare, that the rights hereby asserted are of the natural right of mankind, and that if any act shall be hereafter passed to repeal the present, or to narrow its operation, such act will be an infringement of natural right.[5]

Subject and Comment: **Hands of Power**

Jefferson: What an effort, my dear sir, of bigotry in politics and religion have we gone through! The barbarians really flattered themselves they should be able to bring back the times of vandalism when ignorance put everything into the hands of power and priestcraft.[6]

Subject and Comment: **Religion Lies Solely Between Man and God**

Jefferson: The affectionate sentiments of esteem and approbation which you are so good as to express towards me, on behalf of the Danbury Baptist Association, give me the highest satisfaction.

My duties dictate a faithful and zealous pursuit of the interest of my constituents, and in proportion as they are persuaded of my fidelity to those duties, the discharge of them becomes more and more pleasing.

Believing with you that religion is a matter which lies solely between man and his God, that he owes account to none other for his faith or his worship, that the legislative powers of government reach actions only, and not opinions, I contemplate with

[5] From the Religious Freedom Act of the Assembly of Virginia.
[6] Letter to Joseph Priestly, March 21, 1801.

sovereign reverence that act of the whole American people which declared that their legislature should "make no law respecting an establishment of religion, or prohibiting the free exercise thereof," thus building a wall of separation between Church and State. Adhering to this expression of the supreme will of the nation in behalf of the rights of conscience, I shall see with sincere satisfaction the progress of those sentiments which tend to restore to man all his natural rights, convinced he has no natural right in opposition to his social duties.[7]

Subject and Comment: **Priests As Enemies of the Mind**

JEFFERSON: An opposition, in the meantime, has been got up. That of our alma mater, William and Mary, is not of much weight. She must descend into the secondary rank of academies of preparation for the University. The serious enemies are the priests of the different religious sects, to whose spells on the human mind its improvement is ominous. Their pulpits are now resounding with denunciations against the appointment of Dr. Cooper, whom they charge as a monotheist in opposition to their tritheism. Hostile as these sects are, in every other point, to one another they unite in maintaining their mystical theogony against those who believe there is one God only. The Presbyterian clergy are loudest; the most intolerant of all sects, the most tyrannical and ambitious; ready at the word of the lawgiver, if such a word could be now obtained, to put the torch to the pile, and to rekindle in this virgin hemisphere, the flames in which their oracle Calvin consumed the poor Servetus, because he could not find in his Euclid the proposition which has demonstrated that three are one and one is three, nor subscribed to that of Calvin, that magistrates have a right to exterminate all heretics to Calvinistic Creed. They pant to re-establish, by law, that holy inquisition, which they can now only infuse into public opinion. We have most unwisely committed to the hierophants

[7] Letter to Danbury Baptist Association, 1802.

of our particular superstition, the direction of public opinion, that lord of the universe. We have given them stated and privileged days to collect and catechise us, opportunities of delivering their oracles to the people in mass, and of moulding their minds as wax in the hollow of their hands. But in despite of their fulminations against endeavors to enlighten the general mind, to improve the reason of the people, and encourage them in the use of it, the liberality of this State will support this institution, and give fair play to the cultivation of reason. Can you ever find a more eligible occasion of visiting once more your native country, than that of accompanying Mr. Correa, and of seeing with him this beautiful and hopeful institution in ovo?[8]

Subject and Comment: **Religious Creeds Bane and Ruin of Christian Church**

Jefferson: You asked my opinion on the items of doctrine in you catechism. I have never permitted myself to mediate a specified creed. These formulas have been the bane and ruin of the Christian church, its own fatal invention, which, through so many ages, made of Christendom a slaughter-house, and at this day divides it into casts of inextinguishable hatred to one another. Witness present internecine rage of all sects against the Unitarian. The religions of antiquity had no particular formulas or creed. Those of the modern world none, except those of the religionists calling themselves Christians, and even among these the Quakers have none. And hence, alone, the harmony, the quiet, the brotherly affections, the exemplary and unschismatising society of Friends, and I hope the Unitarians, will follow their happy example.[9]

[JAMES MADISON: One of the authors of The Federalist papers. Called by historians the "Father of the Constitution." Fourth President of the United States.]

[8] Letter to William Short, April 13, 1820.
[9] Letter to Thomas Wittemore, June 5, 1822.

18 /

Subject and Comment: **Pride, Ignorance, and Knavery Among the Priesthood**

Madison: If the Church of England had been the established and general religion in all the northern colonies as it has been among us here, and uninterrupted tranquility had prevailed throughout the continent, it is clear to me that slavery and subjection might and would have been gradually insinuated among us. Union of religious sentiments begets a surprising confidence, and ecclesiastical establishments tend to great ignorance and corruption; all of which facilitate the execution of mischievous projects.

I want again to breathe your free air. I expect it will mend my constitution and confirm my principles. I have indeed as good an atmosphere at home as the climate will allow; but have nothing to brag of as to the state and liberty of my country. Poverty and luxury prevail among all sorts; pride, ignorance, and knavery among the priesthood, and vice and wickedness among the laity. This is bad enough, but it is not the worst I have to tell you. That diabolical, hell-conceived principle of persecution rages among some; and to their eternal infamy, the clergy can furnish their quota of imps for such business. This vexes me the worst of anything whatever. There are at this time in the adjacent country not less than five or six well-meaning men in jail for publishing their religious sentiments, which in the main are very orthodox. I have neither patience to hear, talk, or think of anything relative to this matter; for I have squabbled and scolded, abused and ridiculed, so long about it to little purpose, that I am without common patience. So I must beg you to pity me, and pray for liberty of conscience to all.[10]

Subject and Comment: **Great Barriers, Tyrants, Slaves, Intermeddlers, and Torrents of Blood**

Madison: We, the subscribers, citizens of the said Commonwealth, having taken into serious

[10] Letter to William Bradford, Jr., January 24, 1774.

consideration, a Bill printed by order of the last Session of General Assembly, entitled "A Bill establishing a provision for Teachers of the Christian Religion," and conceiving that the same, if finally armed with the sanctions of law, will be a dangerous abuse of power, are bound as faithful members of a Free State, to remonstrate against it, and to declare the reasons by which we are determined. We remonstrate against the said Bill.

1. Because we hold it for a fundamental and undeniable truth, "that Religion or the duty which we owe to our Creator and the Manner of discharging it, can be directed only by reason and conviction, not by force or violence." The Religion then of every man must be left to the conviction and conscience of every man; and it is the right of every man to exercise it as these may dictate. This right is in its nature an unalienable right. It is unalienable; because the opinion of men, depending only on the evidence contemplated by their own minds, cannot follow the dictates of other men: It is unalienable also because what is here a right towards men, is a duty towards the Creator. It is the duty of every man to render to the Creator such homage, and such only, as he believes to be acceptable to him. This duty is precedent both in order of time and degree of obligation, to the claims of Civil Society. Before any man can be considered as a member of Civil Society, he must be considered as a subject of the Governor of the Universe: And if a member of Civil Society, who enters into any subordinate Association, must always do it with a reservation of his duty to the general authority; much more must every man who becomes a member of any particular Civil Society, do it with a saving of his allegiance to the Universal Sovereign. We maintain therefore that in matter of Religion, no man's right is abridged by the institution of Civil Society, and that Religion is wholly exempt from its cognizance. True it is, that no other rule exists, by which any question which may divide a Society, can be ultimately determined, but the will of the majority; but it is also true, that the majority may trespass on the rights of

the minority.

2. Because if religion be exempt from the authority of the Society at large, still less can it be subject to that of the Legislative Body. The latter are but the creatures and vicegerents [sic] of the former. Their jurisdiction is both derivative and limited: it is limited with regard to the coordinate departments, more necessarily is it limited with regard to the constituents. The preservation of a free government requires not merely, that the metes and bounds which separate each department of power may be invariably maintained; but more especially, that neither of them be suffered to over-leap the great Barrier which defends the rights of the people. The Rulers who are guilty of such an encroachment, exceed the comission from which they derive their authority, and are Tyrants. The People who submit to it are governed by laws made neither by themselves, nor by an authority derived from them, and are slaves.

3. Because, it is proper to take alarm at the first experiment on our liberties. We hold this prudent jealousy to be the first duty of citizens, and one of [the] noblest characteristics of the late Revolution. The freemen of America did not wait till usurped power had strengthened itself by exercise, and entangled the question in precedents. They saw all the consequences in the principle, and they avoided the consequences by denying the principle. We revere this lesson too much, soon to forget it. Who does not see that the same authority which can establish Christianity, in exclusion of all other Religions, may establish with the same ease any particular sect of Christians, in exclusion of all other Sects? That the same authority which can force a citizen to contribute three pence only of his property for the support of any one establishment, may force him to conform to any other establishment in all cases whatsoever?

4. Because, the bill violates that equality which ought to be the basis of every law, and which is more indispensible, in proportion as the validity or expediency of any law is more liable to be impeached. If "all men are by nature equally free

and independent," all men are to be considered as entering into Society on equal conditions; as relinquishing no more, and therefore retaining no less, one than another, of their natural rights. Above all are they to be considered as retaining an "equal title to the free exercise of Religion according to the dictates of conscience." Whilst we assert for ourselves a freedom to embrace, to profess, and to observe the Religion which we believe to be of divine origin, we cannot deny an equal freedom to those whose minds have not yet yielded to the evidence which has convinced us. If this freedom be abused, it is an offence against God, not against man: To God, therefore, not to man, must an account of it be rendered. As the Bill violates equality by subjecting some to peculiar burdens; so it violates the same principle, by granting to others peculiar exemptions. Are the Quakers and Menonists the only sects who think a compulsive support of their religions unnecessary and unwarrantable? Can their piety alone be intrusted with the care of public worship? Ought their Religions to be endowed above all others, with extraordinary privileges, by which proselytes may be enticed from all others? We think too favorable of the justice and good sense of these denominations, to believe that they either covet pre-eminences over their fellow citizens, or that they will be seduced by them, from the common opposition to the measure.

5. Because the bill implies either that the Civil Magistrate is a competent Judge of Religious truth; or that he may employ Religion as an engine of Civil policy. The first is an arrogant pretension falsified by the contradictory opinions of Rulers in all ages, and throughout the world: The second an unhallowed perversion of the means of salvation.

6. Because the establishment proposed by the Bill is not requisite for the support of the Christian Religion. To say that it is, is a contradiction to the Christian Religion itself; for every page of it disavows a dependence on the powers of this world: it is a contradiction to the fact; for it is known that this Religion both existed and flourished, not only without the support of human laws, but

in spite of every opposition from them; and not
only during the period of miraculous aid, but long
after it had been left to its own evidence, and
the ordinary care of Providence: Nay, it is a contradiction in terms; for a Religion not invented by
human policy, must have pre-existed and been supported, before it was established by human policy.
It is moreover to weaken in those who profess this
Religion a pious confidence in its innate excellence,
and the patronage of its Author; and to foster in
those who still reject it, a suspicion that its friends
are too conscious of its fallacies, to trust it to
its own merits.

7. Because experience witnesseth that ecclesiastical establishments, instead of maintaining the purity
and efficacy of Religion, have had a contrary operation. During almost fifteen centuries, has the legal
establishment of Christianity been on trial. What
have been its fruits? More or less in all places,
pride and indolence in the Clergy; ignorance and
servility in the laity; in both superstition, bigotry
and persecution. Enquire of the Teachers of Christianity for the ages in which it appeared in its greatest lustre; those of every sect, point to the ages
prior to its incorporation with Civil policy. Propose
a restoration of this primitive state in which its
Teachers depended on the voluntary rewards of
their flocks; many of them predict its downfall.
On which side ought their testimony to have greatest
weight, when for or when against their interests?

8. Because the establishment in question is not
necessary for the support of Civil Government.
If it be urged as necessary for the support of Civil
Government only as it is a means of supporting
Religion, and it be not necessary for the latter
purpose, it cannot be necessary for the former.
If Religion be not within [the] cognizance of Civil
Government, how can its legal establishment be
said to be necessary to civil Government? What
influence in fact have ecclesiastical establishments
had on Civil Society? In some instances they have
been seen to erect a spiritual tyranny on the ruins
of Civil authority; in many instances they have
been seen upholding the thrones of political tyranny;

in no instance have they been seen the guardians of the liberties of the people. Rulers who wished to subvert the public liberty may have found an established clergy convenient auxiliaries. A just government, instituted to secure and perpetuate it, needs them not. Such a government will be best supported by protecting every citizen in the enjoyment of his Religion with the same equal hand which protects his person and his property; by neither invading the equal rights of any Sect, nor suffering any Sect to invade those of another.

9. Because the proposed establishment is a departure from that generous policy, which, offering an asylum to the persecuted and oppressed of every Nation and Religion, promised a lustre to our country, and an accession to the number of its citizens. What a melancholy mark is the Bill of sudden degeneracy? Instead of holding forth an asylum to the persecuted, it is itself a signal of persecution. It degrades from the equal rank of Citizens all those whose opinions in Religion do not bend to those of the Legislative authority. Distant as it may be, in its present form, from the Inquisition it differs from it only in degree. The one is the first step, the other the last in the career of intolerance. The magnanimous suffer-er under this cruel scourge in foreign Regions, must view the Bill as a Beacon on our Coast, warning him to seek some other haven, where liberty and philanthropy in their due extent may offer a more certain repose from his troubles.

10. Because, it will have a like tendency to banish our Citizens. The allurements presented by other situations are every day thinning their number. To superadd a fresh motive to emigration, by revoking the liberty which they now enjoy, would be the same species of folly which has dishonored and depopulated flourishing kingdoms.

11. Because, it will destroy that moderation and harmony which the forbearance of our laws to intermeddle with Religion, has produced amongst its several sects. Torrents of blood have been spilt in the old world, by vain attempts of the secular arm to extinguish Religious discord, by proscribing

all difference in Religious opinions. Time has at
length revealed the true remedy. Every relaxation
of narrow and rigorous policy, wherever it has been
tried, has been found to assuage the disease. The
American Theatre has exhibited proofs, that equal
and complete liberty, if it does not wholly eradicate
it, sufficiently destroys its malignant influence on
the health and prosperity of the State. If with the
salutary effects of this system under our own eyes,
we begin to contract the bonds of Religious freedom, we know no name that will too severely re-
proach our folly. At least let warning be taken
at the first fruits of the threatened innovation.
The very appearance of the Bill has transformed
that "Christian forbearance, love and charity," which
of late mutually prevailed, into animosities and
jealousies, which may not soon be appeased. What
mischiefs may not be dreaded should this enemy
to the public quiet be armed with the force of
law?

12. Because, the policy of the Bill is adverse
to the diffusion of the light of Christianity. The
first wish of those who enjoy this precious gift,
ought to be that it may be imparted to the whole
race of mankind. Compare the number of those
who have as yet received it with the number still
remaining under the dominion of false Religions;
and how small is the former! Does the policy of
the Bill tend to lessen the disproportion? No; it
at once discourages those who are strangers to
the light of [revelation] from coming into the Region
of it; and countenances, by example the nations
who continue in darkness, in shutting out those
who might convey it to them. Instead of levelling
as far as possible, every obstacle to the victorious
progress of truth, the Bill with an ignoble and un-
christian timidity would circumscribe it, with a
wall of defence, against the encroachments of error.

13. Because attempts to enforce by legal sanctions, acts obnoxious to so great a proportion of
Citizens, tend to enervate the laws in general,
and to slacken the bands of Society. If it be difficult
to execute any law which is not generally deemed
necessary or salutary, what must be the case where

it is deemed invalid and dangerous? And what may be the effect of so striking an example of impotency in the Government, on its general authority.

14. Because a measure of such singular magnitude and delicacy ought not to be imposed, without the clearest evidence that it is called for by a majority of citizens: and no satisfactory method is yet proposed by which the voice of the majority in this case may be determined, or its influence secured. "The people of the respective counties are indeed requested to signify their opinion respecting the adoption of the Bill to the next Session of the Assembly." But the representation must be made equal, before the voice either of the Representatives or of the Counties, will be that of the people. Our hope is that neither of the former will, after due consideration, espouse the dangerous principle of the Bill. Should the event disappoint us, it will still leave us in full confidence, that a fair appeal to the latter will reverse the sentence against our liberties.

15. Because, finally, "the equal right of every citizen to the free exercise of his Religion according to the dictates of conscience" is held by the same tenure with all our other rights. If we recur to its origin, it is equally the gift of nature; if we weigh its importance, it cannot be less dear to us; if we consult the Declaration of those rights which pertain to the good people of Virginia, as the "basis and foundation of Government," it is enumerated with equal solemnity, or rather studied emphasis. Either then, we must say, that the will of the Legislature is the only measure of their authority; and that in the plenitude of this authority, they may sweep away all our fundamental rights; or, that they are bound to leave this particular right untouched and sacred: Either we must say, that they may control the freedom of the press, may abolish the trial by jury, may swallow up the Executive and Judiciary Powers of the State; nay that they may despoil us of our very right to suffrage, and erect themselves into an independent and hereditary assembly: or we must say, that they have no authority to enact into law the Bill under consideration. We the subscribers say, that the Gen-

eral Assembly of this Commonwealth have no such
authority: And that no effort may be omitted on
our part against so dangerous an usurpation, we
oppose to it, this remonstrance; earnestly praying,
as we are in duty bound, that the Supreme Lawgiver
of the Universe, by illuminating those to whom
it is addressed, may on the one hand, turn their
councils from every act which would affront his
holy prerogative, or violate the trust committed
to them: and on the other, guide them into every
measure which may be worthy of his [blessing may
re]dound to their own praise, and may establish
more firmly the liberties, the prosperity, and the
Happiness of the Commonwealth.[11]

Subject and Comment: Not a Shadow of a Right for Government to Intermeddle with Religion

Madison: The honorable member has introduced
the subject of religion. Religion is not guarded
- there is no bill of rights declaring that religion
should be secure. Is a bill of rights a security for
Religion? Would the bill of rights, in this state,
exempt the people from paying for the support
of one particular sect, if such sect were exclusively
established by law? If there were a majority of
one sect, a bill of rights would be poor protection
for liberty. Happily for the states, they enjoy the
utmost freedom of religion. This freedom arises
from that multiplicity of sects, which pervades
America, and which is the best and only security
for religious liberty in any society. For where there
is such a variety of sects, there cannot be a majority
of any one sect to oppress and persecute the rest.
Fortunately for the commonwealth, a majority of
the people are decidedly against any exclusive
establishment - I believe it to be so in the other
states. There is not a shadow of a right in the
general government to intermeddle with religion.
Its least interference with it, would be a most
flagrant usurpation. I can appeal to my uniform
conduct on this subject, that I have warmly supported
religious freedom. It is better that this security

[11] Madison's **Memorial and Remonstrance** of 1785. Written against
the Religious Assessment Bill of 1785 in Virginia.

should be depended upon from the general legislature, than from one particular state. A particular state might concur in one religious project. But the United States abound in such a variety of sects, that it is a strong security against religious persecution, and it is sufficient to authorize the conclusion, that no one sect will ever be able to out-number or depress the rest.[12]

Subject and Comment: **Jews and Christians Equally Protected**

Madison: I have received your letter of the 7th inst. with the Discourse delivered at the Consecration of the Hebrew Synagogue at Savannah, for which you will please to accept my thanks.

The history of the Jews must forever be interesting. The modern part of it is, at the same time so little generally known, that every ray of light on the subject has its value.

Among the features peculiar to the Political system of the United States, is the perfect equality of rights which it secures to every religious Sect. And it is particularly pleasing to observe in the good citizenship of such as have been most distrusted and oppressed elsewhere, a happy illustration of the safety and success of this experiment of a just and benignant policy. Equal laws protecting equal rights, are found as they ought to be presumed, the best guarantee of loyalty and love of country; as well as best calculated to cherish that mutual respect and good will among Citizens of every religious denomination which are necessary to social harmony and most favorable to the advancement of truth. The account you give of the Jews of your Congregation brings them fully within the scope of these observations.[13]

Subject and Comment: **Freedom of Religion Improves the Priesthood**

Madison: It was the Universal opinion of the Century

[12] Madison's journals re. Constitutional Convention, 1788.
[13] Letter to Jacob De La Motta, August, 1820.

preceding the last, that Civil Government could not stand without the prop of a Religious establishment, and that the Christian religion itself, would perish if not supported by a legal provision for its Clergy. The experiment of Virginia conspicuously corroborates the disproof of both opinions. The Civil Government, tho' bereft of everything like an associated hierarchy, possesses the requisite stability and performs its functions with complete success whilst the number, the industry, and the morality of the Priesthood, and the devotion of the people have been manifestly increased by the total separation of the Church and State.[14]

The world is my country,
All mankind are my brethren,
To do good is my religion,
I believe in one God and no more.
Thomas Paine

[THOMAS PAINE: Fighter against atheism and for human freedom. Writing of what he called "the times that try men's souls," he probably did more than anyone to galvanize Americans into open defiance of British rule. George Washington said of Paine that he worked "a powerful change in the minds of many men." Andrew Jackson told a friend: "Thomas Paine needs no monument made by hands; he has erected a monument in the hearts of all lovers of liberty." Author of Common Sense, The Age of Reason, The Rights of Man, et al.]

Subject and Comment: **A Person Can Be His or Her Own Church. Formal Churches Terrify and Enslave. Infidelity Is Saying What You Believe You Don't.**

Paine: As several of my colleagues, and others of my fellow-citizens of France, have given me the example of making their voluntary and individual profession of faith, I also will make mine; and I do this with all that sincerity and frankness with

[14]Letter to Robert Walsh, March 2, 1819.

which the mind of man communicates with itself.

I believe in the equality of man; and I believe that religious duties consist in doing justice, loving mercy, and endeavoring to make our fellow-creatures happy.

But, lest it should be supposed that I believe many other things in addition to these, I shall, in the progress of this work, declare the things I do not believe, and my reason for not believing them.

I do not believe in the creed professed by the Jewish Church, by the Roman Church, by the Greek Church, by the Turkish Church, by the Protestant Church, nor by any church that I know of. My own mind is my own church.

All national institutions of churches, whether Jewish, Christian or Turkish, appear to me no other than human inventions, set up to terrify and enslave mankind, and monopolize power and profit.

I do not mean by this declaration to condemn those who believe otherwise; they have the same right to their belief as I have to mine. But it is necessary to the happiness of man that he be mentally faithful to himself. Infidelity does not consist in believing, or in disbelieving; it consists in professing to believe what he does not believe.

It is impossible to calculate the moral mischief, if I may so express it, that mental lying has produced in society. When a man has so far corrupted and prostituted the chastity of his mind as to subscribe his professional belief to things he does not believe he has prepared himself for the commission of every other crime.

He takes up the trade of a priest for the sake of gain, and in order to qualify himself for that trade he begins with a perjury. Can we conceive any thing more destructive of morality than this?

Soon after I had published the pamphlet "Common Sense," in America, I saw the exceeding probability that a revolution in the system of government would be followed by a revolution in the system of religion. The adulterous connection of church and state, wherever it has taken place, whether Jewish, Christian or Turkish, had so effectually prohibited by pains and penalties every discussion upon established creeds, and upon first principles of religion, that until the system of government should be changed, those subjects could not be brought fairly and openly before the world; but that whenever this should be done, a revolution in the system of religion would follow. Human inventions and priestcraft would be detected; and man would return to the pure, unmixed and unadulterated belief in one God, and no more.[15]

Subject and Comment: **Church of the Out-of-Doors. Sabbath Day In Connecticut**

Paine: The word Sabbath, means REST; that is, cessation from labor, but the stupid Blue Laws of Connecticut make a labor of rest, for they oblige a person to sit still from sunrise to sunset on a Sabbath-day, which is hard work. Fanaticism made those laws, and hypocrisy pretends to reverence them, for where such laws prevail hypocrisy will prevail also.

One of those laws says, "No person shall run on a Sabbath-day, nor walk in his garden, no elsewhere; but reverently to and from meeting." These fanatical hypocrites forgot that God dwells not in temples made with hands, and that the earth is full of His glory.

One of the finest scenes and subjects of religious contemplation is to walk into the woods and fields, and survey the works of the God of the Creation. The wide expanse of heaven, the earth covered with verdure, the lofty forest, the waving corn, the magnificent roll of mighty rivers, and the murmuring melody of the cheerful brooks, are scenes that inspire the mind with gratitude and delight.

But this the gloomy Calvinist of Connecticut must not behold on a Sabbath-day. Entombed within the walls of his dwelling, he shuts from his view the Temple of Creation. The sun shines no joy to him. The gladdening voice of nature calls on him in vain. He is deaf, dumb and blind to everything

15 From **The Age of Reason.**

around that God has made. Such is the Sabbath-day in Connecticut.

From whence could come this miserable notion of devotion? It comes from the gloominess of the Calvinistic creed. If men love darkness rather than light, because their works are evil, the ulcerated mind of a Calvinist, who sees God only in terror, and sits brooding over the scenes of hell and damnation, can have no joy in beholding the glories of the creation. Nothing in that mighty and wondrous system accords with his principles or his devotion.

He sees nothing there that tells him that God created millions on purpose to be damned, and that the children of a span long are born to burn forever in hell. The creation preaches a different doctrine to this. We there see that the care and goodness of God is extended impartially over all the creatures He has made. The worm of the earth shares His protection equally with the elephant of the desert. The grass that springs beneath our feet grows by his bounty as well as the cedars of Lebanon.

Everything in the creation reproaches the Calvinist with unjust ideas of God, and disowns the hardness and ingratitude of his principles. Therefore he shuns the sight of them on a Sabbath-day. [From "The Age of Reason"]

Subject and Comment: **The Sacred, Profane, and Ecclesiastical. The Word of God? Miracles?**

Paine: It has been customary to class history into three divisions, distinguished by the names of Sacred, Profane and Ecclesiastical. By the first is meant the Bible; by the second, the history of nations, of men and things; and by the third, the history of the church and its priesthood.

Nothing is more easy than to give names, and, therefore, mere names signify nothing unless they lead to the discovery of some cause for which that name was given. For example, Sunday is the name given the first day of the week, in the English language, and it is the same in the Latin, that is, it has the same meaning (Dies solis), and also in the German and also in several other languages.

Why then was this name given to that day? Because it was the day dedicated by the ancient world to the luminary which in the English we call the Sun, and therefore the day Sun-day, or the day of the Sun; as in the like manner we call the second day Monday, the day dedicated to the Moon.

Here the name Sunday leads to the cause of its being called so, and we have visible evidence of the fact, because we behold the Sun from whence the name comes; but this is not the case when we distinguish one part of history from another by the name of Sacred.

All histories have been written by men. We have no evidence, nor any cause to believe, that any have been written by God. That part of the Bible called the Old Testament, is the history of the Jewish nation, from the time of Abraham, which begins in Genesis xi, to the downfall of that nation by Nebuchadnezzar, and is no more entitled to be called sacred than any other history. It is altogether the contrivance of priestcraft that has given it that name. So far from its being sacred, it has not the appearance of being true in many of the things it relates.

It must be better authority than a book which any imposter might make, as Mahomet made the Koran, to make a thoughtful man believe that the sun and moon stood still, or that Moses and Aaron turned the Nile, which is larger that the Delaware, into blood; and that the Egyptian magicians did the same. These things have too much the appearance of romance to be believed for fact.

It would be of use to inquire, and ascertain the time, when that part of the Bible called the Old Testament first appeared. From all that can be collected there was no such book till after the Jews returned from captivity in Babylon, and that is the work of the Pharisees of the Second Temple. How they came to make Kings xix and Isaiah xxxvii word for word alike, can only be accounted for by their having no plan to go by, and not knowing what they were about.

The same is the case with respect to the last

verses in 2 Chronicles, and the first verses of Ezra; they also are word for word alike, which shows that the Bible has been put together at random.

But besides these things there is great reason to believe we have been imposed upon with respect to the antiquity of the Bible, and especially with respect to the books ascribed to Moses. Herodotus, who is called the father of history, and is the most ancient historian whose works have reached to our time, and who traveled into Egypt, conversed with the priests, historians, astronomers and learned men of that country, for the purpose of obtaining all the information of it he could, and who gives an account of the ancient state of it, makes no mention of such a man as Moses, though the Bible makes him to have been the greatest hero there, nor of any one circumstance mentioned in the book of Exodus respecting Egypt, such as turning the rivers into blood, the dust into lice, the death of the first born throughout all the land of Egypt, the passage of the Red Sea, the drowning of Pharaoh and all his host, things which could not have been a secret in Egypt, and must have been generally known, had they been facts; and, therefore, as no such things were known in Egypt, nor any such man as Moses at the time Herodotus was there, which is about 2,200 years ago, it shows that the account of these things in the books ascribed to Moses is a made story of later times; that is, after the return of the Jews from the Babylonian captivity, and that Moses is not the author of the books ascribed to him.

With respect to cosmogony, or account of the Creation, in Genesis i, of the Garden of Eden in chapter ii, and of what is called the Fall of Man in chapter iii, there is something concerning them we are not historically acquainted with. In none of the books of the Bible, after Genesis, are any of these things mentioned of even alluded to.

How is this to be accounted for? The obvious inference is that either they were not known, or not believed to be facts, by the writers of the other books of the Bible, and that Moses is not the author of the chapters where these accounts

34 /

are given.

* * *

There is good reason to believe we have been in great error with respect to the antiquity of the Bible, as well as imposed upon by its contents. Truth ought to be the object of every man; for without truth there can be no real happiness to a thoughtful mind, or any assurance of happiness hereafter. It is the duty of man to obtain all the knowledge he can, and then make the best use of it.[16]

Subject and Comment: **Fables and Facts. Councils and Contradictions.**

Paine: "Great is Diana of the Ephesians," was the cry of the people of Ephesus (Acts xix, 28); and the cry of "our holy religion" has been the cry of superstition in some instances, and of hypocrisy in others, from that day to this.

The Brahmin, the follower of Zoroaster, the Jew, the Mahometan, the Church of Rome, the Greek Church, the Protestant Church, split into several hundred contradictory sectaries, preaching in some instances damnation against each other, all cry out, "our holy religion."

The Calvinist, who damns children of a span long to hell to burn forever for the glory of God (and this is called Christianity), and the Universalist who preaches that all shall be saved and none shall be damned (and this is also called Christianity), boast alike of their holy religion and their Christian faith.

Something more therefore is necessary than mere cry and wholesale assertion, and that something is truth; and as inquiry is the road to truth, he that is opposed to inquiry is not a friend to truth.

The God of truth is not the God of fable; when, therefore, any book is introduced into the world as the Word of God, and made a groundwork for religion, it ought to be scrutinized more than other books to see if it bear evidence of being what it is called. Our reverence to God demands that

[16]From **Prospect Papers** of 1804.

we do this, lest we ascribe to God what is not His and our duty to ourselves demands it lest we take fable for fact, and rest our hope of salvation on a false foundation.

It is not our calling a book holy that makes it so, any more than our calling a religion holy that entitles it to the name. Inquiry therefore is necessary in order to arrive at truth. But inquiry must have some principle to proceed on, some standard to judge by, superior to human authority.

When we survey the works of creation, the revolutions of the planetary system, and the whole economy of what is called nature, which is no other than the laws the Creator has prescribed to matter, we see unerring order and universal harmony reigning throughout the whole. No one part contradicts another. The sun does not run against the moon, nor the moon against the sun, nor the planets against each other. Everything keeps its appointed time and place.

This harmony in the works of God is so obvious, that the farmer of the field, though he cannot calculate eclipses, is as sensible of it as the philosophical astronomer. He sees the God of order in every part of the visible universe.

Here, then, is the standard to which everything must be brought that pretends to be the work or Word of God, and by this standard it must be judged, independently of anything and everything that man can say or do. His opinion is like a feather in the scale compared with the standard that God Himself has set up.

It is, therefore, by this standard that the Bible and all other books pretending to be the Word of God (and there are many of them in the world) must be judged, and not by the opinions of men or the decrees of ecclesiastical councils. These have been so contradictory that they have often rejected in one council what they had voted to be the Word of God in another; and admitted what had been before rejected.

In this state of uncertainty in which we are, and which is rendered still more uncertain by the numerous contradictory sectaries that have sprung up since the time of Luther and Calvin, what is man to do? The answer is easy. Begin at the root - begin with he Bible itself. Examine it with the utmost strictness. It is our duty so to do.

Compare the parts with each other, and the whole with the harmonious, magnificent order that reigns throughout the visible universe, and the result will be, that if the same Almighty wisdom that created the universe dictated also the Bible, the Bible will be as harmonious and as magnificent in all its parts and in the whole as the universe is.

But, if instead of this, the parts are found to be discordant, contradicting in one place what is said in another (as in 2 Sam. xxiv, 1, and 1 Chron. xxi, 1, where the same action is ascribed to God in one book and to Satan in the other), abounding also in idle and obscene stories, and representing the Almighty as a passionate, whimsical Being, continually changing His mind, and making and unmaking His own works as if he did not know what He was about, we may take it for certainty that the Creator of the Universe is not the author of such a book, that it is not the Word of God, and that to call it so is to dishonor His name.

The Quakers, who are a people more moral and regular in their conduct than the people of other sectaries, and generally allowed so to be, do not hold the Bible to be the Word of God. They call it a history of the times, and a bad history it is, and also a history of bad men and of bad actions, and abounding with bad examples.

For several centuries past the dispute has been about doctrines. It is now about fact. Is the Bible the Word of God, or is it not? For until this point is established, no doctrine drawn from the Bible can afford real consolation to man, and he ought to be careful he does not mistake delusion for truth. This is a case that concerns all men alike.

There has always existed in Europe, and also in America, since its establishment, a numerous description of men (I do not here mean the Quakers) who did not, and do not believe the Bible to be the Word of God. These men never formed themselves into an established society, but are to be found in all the sectaries that exist, and are more numerous than any, perhaps equal to all, and are daily increasing. From Deus, the Latin word for God, they have been denominated Deists, that is believers in God. It is the most honorable appellation that can be given to man, because it is derived immediately from the Deity. It is not an artificial name like Episcopalian, Presbyterian, etc., but is a name of sacred signification, and to revile it is to revile the name of God.

Since then there is so much doubt and uncertainty about the Bible, some asserting and others denying it to be the Word of God, it is best that the whole matter come out. It is necessary for the information of the world that it should.

A better time cannot offer than while the Government, patronizing no one sect or opinion in preference to another, protects equally the rights of all; and certainly every man must spurn the idea of an ecclesiastical tyranny, engrossing the rights of the press, and holding it free only for itself.

While the terrors of the Church, and the tyranny of the State, hung like a pointed sword over Europe, men were commanded to believe what the Church told them, or go to the stake. All inquiries into the authenticity of the Bible were shut out by the Inquisition. We ought therefore to suspect that a great mass of information respecting the Bible, and the introduction of it into the world, has been suppressed by the united tyranny of Church and State, for the purpose of keeping people in ignorance, and which ought to be known.

The Bible has been received by the Protestants on the authority of the Church of Rome, and on no other authority. It is she that has said it is the Word of God. We do not admit the authority of that Church with respect to its pretended infallibility, its manufactured miracles, its setting itself up to forgive sins, its amphibious doctrine of transubstantiation, etc.; and we ought to be watchful with respect to any book introduced by her, or her ecclesiastical councils, and called by her the Word of God: and the more so, because it was by propagating that belief and supporting it by fire and faggot that she kept up her temporal power.[17]

[JOHN ADAMS: Ideas influenced Jefferson, and were reflected in the Declaration of Independence. Served in the Continental Congress. Second President of the United States. Father of John Quincy Adams, our sixth President.]

Subject and Comment: **Exquisite Torture and Pertinacious Spirit. The Priest and the Great Whore.**

Adams: Tyranny in every form, and shape, and appearance was their disdain and abhorrence; no fear of punishment, nor even death itself in exquisite tortures, had been sufficient to conquer that steady, manly, pertinacious spirit with which they had opposed the tyrants of those days in church and state.

They are very far from being enemies to monarchy; and they knew as well as any men, the just regard and honor that is due the character of dispenser of the mysteries of the gospel of grace. But they saw clearly, that popular powers must be placed as a guard, a control, a balance, to the powers of the monarch and the priest, in every government, or else it would soon become the man of sin, the whore of Babylon, the mystery of iniquity, a great and detestable system of fraud, violence, and usurpation.[18]

Subject and Comment: **Frightful Engines and Ecclesiastical Councils**

Adams: The frightful engines of ecclesiastical councils, of diabolical malice and Calvinistical good-nature never failed to terrify me exceedingly whenever I thought of preaching. But the point is now determined, and I shall have liberty to think for myself without molesting others or being molested myself. Write to me the first good opportunity, and tell me freely whether you approve my conduct.[19]

[17] From **Prospect** papers of 1804.
[18] **Boston Gazette,** August, 1765.
[19] **Novanglus** papers, 1774.

Subject and Comment: **Most Bloody Religion. Millions of Fables.**

Adams: Christianity, you will say, was a fresh revelation. I will deny this. As I understand the Christian religion, it was, and is, a revelation. But how has it happened that millions of fables, tales, legends, have been blended with both Jewish and Christian revelation that have made them the most bloody religion that ever existed? How has it happened that all the fine arts, architecture, painting, sculpture, statuary, music, poetry, and oratory, have been prostituted, from the creation of the world, to the sordid and detestable purposes of superstition and fraud?[20]

Subject and Comment: **Man's Hand in the Word of God**

Adams: What havoc has been made of books through every century of the Christian era? Where are fifty gospels condemned as spurious by the bull of Pope Gelasius? Where are the forty wagon-loads of Hebrew manuscripts burned in France, by order of another pope, because suspected of heresy? Remember the index expurgatorius, the inquisition, the stake, the axe, the halter, and the guillotine; and, oh, horrible, the rack? This is as bad, if not worse, than a slow fire. Nor should the Lion's Mouth be forgotten.[21]

Subject and Comment: **Truth and Dogmas Don't Mix**

Adams: Turn our thoughts in the next place, to the characters of learned men. The priesthood have, in all ancient nations, nearly monopolized learning. Read over again all the accounts we have of Hindoos, Chaldeans, Persians, Greeks, Romans, Celts, Teutons, we shall find that priests had all the know-

[20] Letter to F.A. Van der Kemp, December 27, 1816.
[21] Letter to John Taylor; No. 16, 1814.

ledge, and really governed all mankind. Examine
Mohametanism, trace Christianity from its first
promulgation; knowledge has been almost exclusively
confined to the clergy. And, even since the Refor-
ation, when or where has existed a Protestant or
dissenting sect who would tolerate A FREE INQUIR-
Y? The blackest billingsgate, the most ungentlemanly
insolence, the most yahooish brutality is patiently
endured, countenanced, propagated, and applauded.
But touch a solemn truth in collision with a dogma
of a sect, though capable of the clearest proof,
and you will soon find you have disturbed a nest,
and the hornets will swarm about your legs and
hands and fly into your face and eyes.[22]

Subject and Comment: **Horrid Cruelties, Superstitions,
and Hypocrisy. All Good Men Christians.**

Adams: Before I was twelve years of age, I necessarily became a reader of polemical writings of religion,
as well as politics, and for more than seventy years
I have indulged myself in that kind of reading,
as far as the wandering, anxious, and perplexed
kind of life, which Providence has compelled me
to pursue, would admit. I have endeavored to obtain
as much information as I could of all the religions
which have ever existed in the world. Mankind are
by nature religious creatures. I have found no nation
without a religion, nor any people without the belief
of a supreme Being. I have been overwhelmed with
sorrow to see natural love and fear of that Being
wrought upon by politicians to produce the most
horrid cruelties, superstitions, and hypocrisy, from
the sacrifices of Moloch down to those of
Juggernaut, and . . . the kings of Whidah and
Ashantee. The great result of all my researches
has been a most diffusive and comprehensive charity.
I believe with Justin Martyr, that all good men
are Christians, and I believe there have been, and
are, good men in all nations. . . . That you and
I shall meet in a better world, I have no more
doubt than I that we now exist on the same globe.

[22]Letter to John Taylor; No. 31. 1814.

If my natural reason did not convince me of this, Cicero's dream of Scipio, and his essays on friendship and old age, would have been sufficient for the purpose. But Jesus has taught us, that a future state is a social state, when he promised to prepare places in his Father's house of many mansions for his disciples.[23]

[BENJAMIN FRANKLIN: Influential delegate and peacemaker among the delegates to the Constitutional Convention. Suggested that Congress have prayer each day. Inventor, philosopher, and statesman.]

Subject and Comment: **The Lord's Prayer Revised**

Franklin: Father, may all revere thee, and become thy dutiful children and faithful subjects. May thy laws be obeyed on earth, as perfectly as they are in heaven. Provide for us this day, as thou hast hitherto daily done. Forgive us our trespasses, and enable us to forgive those who offend us, Keep us out of temptation, and deliver us from evil.[24]

Subject and Comment: **Respect Them All**

Franklin: I had been religiously educated as a Presbyterian; and though some of the dogmas of that persuasion, such as the eternal decrees of God, election, reprobation, etc., appeared to me unintelligible, others doubtful, and I early absented myself from the public assemblies of the sect, Sunday being my studying day, I never was without some religious principles. I never doubted, for instance, the existence of the Deity; that he made the world, and governed it by his Providence; that the most acceptable service of God was the doing good to man; that our souls are immortal; and that all crime will be punished, and virtue rewarded, either here or hereafter. These I esteemed the essentials of every religion; and, being found in all the religions we had in our country, I respected them all, though with different degrees of respect, as I found them

[23] Letter to Samuel Miller, July 8, 1820.
[24] Cousins, supra, p. 21.

more or less mixed with other articles, which, without any tendency to inspire, promote, or confirm morality, served principally to divide us, and make us unfriendly to one another. This respect to all, with an opinion that the worst had some good effects, induced me to avoid all discourse that might tend to lessen the good opinion another might have of his own religion; and as our province increased in people, and new places of worship were continually wanted, and generally erected by voluntary contribution, my mite for such purpose, whatever might be the sect, was never refused.[25]

Subject and Comment: **One God. Teachings of Jesus Corrupted. All Sects Acceptable.**

Franklin: Here is my creed. I believe in one God, Creator of the Universe. That He governs it by His providence. That He ought to be worshipped. That the most acceptable service we render Him is doing good to His other children. That the soul of man is immortal, and will be treated with justice in another life respecting its conduct in this. These I take to be the principal principles of sound religion, and I regard them as you do in whatever sect I meet with them. As to Jesus of Nazareth, my opinion of whom you particularly desire, I think the system of morals and his religion, as he left them to us, the best the world ever saw or is likely to see; but I apprehend it has received various corrupt changes, and I have, with most of the present dissenters in England, some doubts as to his divinity; though it is a question I do not dogmatize upon, having never studied it, and think it needless to busy myself with it now, when I expect soon an opportunity of knowing the truth with less trouble. I see no harm, however, in it being believed, if that belief has the good consequence, as probably it has, of making his doctrines more respected and better observed; especially as I do not perceive that the Supreme [Being] takes it amiss, by distinguishing the unbelievers in His government of the world with any peculiar marks of His displeasure.

[25] From Franklin's autobiography.

*　　*　　*

All sects here, and we have a great variety, have experienced my good will in assisting them with subscriptions for building their new places of worship; and, as I have never opposed their doctrines, I hope to go out of the world in peace with them all. . . .[26]

Subject and Comment: **United States Created for All Religions**

Franklin: And it being found inconvenient to assemble in the open air, subject to its inclemencies, the building of a house to meet in was no sooner proposed, and persons appointed to received contributions, but sufficient sums were soon received to procure the ground and erect the building, which was one hundred feet long and seventy broad, about the size of Westminster Hall; and the work was carried on with such spirit as to be finished in much shorter time than could have been expected. Both house and ground were vested in trustees, expressly for the use of any preacher of any religious persuasion who might desire to say something to the people at Philadelphia; the design in building not being to accommodate any particular sect, but the inhabitants in general; so that even if the Mufti of Constantinople were to send a missionary to preach Mohammedanism to us, he would find a pulpit at his service.[27]

Subject and Comment: **Liberty for All the World's People**

Franklin: God grant that not only the Love of Liberty but a thorough knowledge of the rights of man may pervade all the nations of the earth, so that a philosopher may set his feet anywhere on its surface and say, "This is my country."[28]

[26] Letter to Ezra Stiles, President of Yale University.
[27] From Franklin's autobiography.
[28] Cousins, supra, p. 43.

44 /

[GEORGE WASHINGTON: The cohesive force ideally
suited to preside at the Constitutional Convention;
and, later, his prestige was of great value in getting
the Constitution radified. Although he had only
five years of formal schooling, he became our first
President and came to be called "The Father of
His Country."]

Subject and Comment: **No Drunks or Cursers Allowed**

The General most earnestly requires, and expects,
a due observance of those articles of war, established
for the government of the army which forbid profane
cursing, swearing and drunkenness; and in like manner
requires and expects, of all officers, and soldiers,
not engaged on actual duty, a punctual attendance
on divine service, to implore the blessings of heaven
upon the means used for our safety and defence.[29]

Subject and Comment: **Providential Goodness and
Christianity**

Washington: While we are zealously performing the
duties of good Citizens and Soldiers we certainly
ought not to be inattentive to the higher duties
of Religion. To the distinguished Character of Pa-
triot, it should be our highest Glory to add the
more distinguished Character of Christian. The signal
instances of providential Goodness which we have
experienced and which have now almost crowned
our labours with complete success, demand from
us in a peculiar manner the warmest returns of
Gratitude and Piety to the Supreme Author of all
Good.[30]

Subject and Comment: **Profaning the Name of God**

Washington: The Name of That Being, from whose
bountiful goodness we are permitted to exist and
enjoy the comforts of life is incessantly imprecated
and profaned in a manner as wanton as it is shock-

[29] General Orders, July 4, 1775.
[30] Valley Forge, May 2, 1778.

ing. For the sake therefore of religion, decency
and order the General hopes and trusts that officers
of every rank will use their influence and authority
to check a vice, which is as unprofitable as it is
wicked and shameful.[31]

Subject and Comment: **Beware Some Acts of Providence**

Washington: I most sincerely condole with you on
your late loss; and doubt not your feeling it in
the most sensible manner; nor do I expect that
human Fortitude, and reason, can so far overcome
natural affection, as to enable us to look with calm-
ness upon losses which distress us although they
are acts of Providence, and in themselves unavoid-
able, ye acquiescence to the divine will is not only
a duty, but is to be aided by every manly exertion
to forget the causes of such uneasiness.[32]

Subject and Comment: **Inscrutable Ways of Providence**

Washington: Your favor of 8th Decr. came safe
to my hands after a considerable delay in its passage. The sentiments you have expressed of me in
this Letter are highly flattering, meriting my warmest acknowledgments, as I have too good an Opinion
of your sincerity and candour to believe that you
are capable of unmeaning professions and speaking
a language foreign from your Heart. The friendship
I ever professed, and felt for you, met with no
diminution from the difference in our political Sentiments. I know the rectitude of my own intentions,
and believing in the sincerity of yours, lamented,
though I did not condemn, your renunciation of
the creed I had adopted. Nor do I think any person,
or power, ought to do it, whilst your conduct is
not opposed to the general Interest of the people
and the measures they are pursuing; the latter,
that is our actions, depending upon ourselves, may
be controlled, while the powers of thinking originating
in higher causes, cannot always be moulded to our

[31] Moore's house, July 29, 1779.
[32] Letter to brother Samuel Washington, August 10, 1777.

wishes.

The determinations of Providence are all ways wise; often inscrutable, and though its decrees appear to bear hard upon us at times is nevertheless meant for gracious purposes; in this light I cannot help viewing your late disappointment; for if you had been permitted to have gone to England, unrestrained even by the rigid oaths which are administered on those occasions your feelings as a husband, Parent, and etc. must have been considerably wounded in the prospect of a long, perhaps lasting separation from your nearest relatives. What then must they have been if the obligation of an oath had left you without a Will? Your hope of being instrumental in restoring Peace would prove as unsubstantial as a mist before the Noon days Sun and would as soon dispel: for believe me, Sir, great Britain understood herself perfectly well in this dispute but did not comprehend America. She meant as Lord Campden in his late speech in Parliament clearly, and explicitly declared, to drive America into rebellion that her own purposes might be more fully answered by it but take this along with it, that this Plan originating in firm belief, founded on misinformation.[33]

Subject and Comment: **Doctrine of Providence**

Washington: It is not a little pleasing, nor less wonderful to contemplate, that after two years manoeuvring and undergoing the strangest vicissitudes that perhaps ever attended any one contest since the creation, both armies are brought back to the very point they set out from and, that that which was the offending party in the beginning is now reduced to the use of the spade and pick axe for defence. The hand of Providence has been so conspicuous in all this, that he must be worse than an infidel that lacks faith, and more than wicked, that has not gratitude enough to acknowledge his obligations but, it will be time enough for me to turn preacher which my present appointment ceases; and therefore I shall add no more on the Doctrine

[33] Letter to Bryan Fairfax, March 1, 1778.

of Providence; but make a tender of my best re-
spects to your good Lady; the Secretary and other
friends, and assure you that with the most perfect
regard I am &c.[34]

Subject and Comment: **Indians Are As One With
Us All**

Washington: Brothers: I am glad you have brought
three of the Children of your principal Chiefs to
be educated with us. I am sure Congress will open
the arms of love to them, and will look upon them
as their own Children, and will have them educated
accordingly. This is a great mark of your confidence
and of your desire to preserve the friendship between
the Two Nations to the end of time, and to become
One people with your Brethren of the United States.
My ears hear with pleasure the other matters you
mention. Congress will be glad to hear them too.
You do well to wish to learn our arts and way
of life, and above all, the religion of Jesus Christ.
These will make you a greater and happier people
than you are. Congress will do every thing they
can to assist you in this wise intention; and to
tie the knot of friendship and union so fast, that
nothing shall ever be able to loose it.[35]

Subject and Comment: **Providence Interposed to
Protect Our Liberties**

Washington: Your affectionate congratulations on
the happy conclusion of the War, and the glorious
prospect now opening to this extensive Country,
cannot but be extremely satisfactory to me.
  Having shared in common, the hardships and dan-
gers of the War with my virtuous fellow Citizens
in the field, as well as with those who on the Lines
have been immediately exposed to the Arts and
Arms of the Enemy, I feel the most lively sentiments
of gratitude to that divine Providence which has
graciously interposed for the protection of our Civil
and Religious Liberties.

[34] Letter to Thomas Nelson, August 20, 1778.
[35] Speech to Indian chiefs, May 12, 1779.

In retiring from the field of Contest to the sweets of private life, I claim no merit, but if in that retirement my most earnest wishes and prayers can be of avail, nothing will exceed the prosperity of our common Country, and the temporal and spiritual felicity of those who are represented in your Address.[36]

Subject and Comment: **Country Saved By Glorious Being**

Washington: Disposed, at every suitable opportunity to acknowledge publicly our infinite obligations to the Supreme Ruler of the Universe for rescuing our Country from the brink of destruction; I cannot fail at this time to ascribe all the honor of our late successes to the same glorious Being. And if my humble exertions have been made in any degree subservient to the execution of the divine purposes, a contemplation of the benediction of Heaven on our righteous Cause, the approbation of my virtuous Countrymen, and the testimony of my own Conscience, will be of sufficient reward and augment my felicity beyond anything which the world can bestow.[37]

Subject and Comment: **Greatest and Best of Beings**

Washington: For the reestablishment of our once violated rights; for the confirmation of our Independence; for the protection of Virtue, Philosophy and Literature: for the present flourishing state of the Sciences, and for the enlarged prospect of human happiness, it is our common duty to pay the tribute of gratitude to the greatest and best of Beings.[38]

Subject and Comment: **Spiritual Tyranny and Religious Persecution**

Washington: If I could have entertained the slightest

[36] Letter of November 10, 1783, to Hackensack minister, et al.
[37] Letter to Reformed German Church, November 27, 1783.
[38] Letter to citizens of Philadelphia, December 13, 1783.

apprehension, that the constitution framed in the convention, where I had the honor to preside, might possibly endanger the religious rights of any ecclesiastical society, certainly I would never have placed my signature to it; and if I could now conceive that the general government might ever be so administered as to render the liberty of conscience insecure, I beg you will be persuaded, that no one would be more zealous than myself to establish effectual barriers against the horrors of spiritual tyranny, and every species of religious persecution. For you doubtless remember, that I have often expressed my sentiments that every man, conducting himself as a good citizen, and being accountable to God alone for his religious opinions, ought to be protected in worshipping the Deity according to the dictates of his own conscience.[39]

Subject and Comment: **Christians Dwelling Together in Charity**

Washington: On this occasion it would ill become me to conceal the joy I have felt, in perceiving the fraternal affection, which appears to increase every day among the friends of genuine religion. It affords edifying prospects, indeed, to see Christians of different denominations dwell together in more charity, and conduct themselves in respect to each other with more Christian-like spirit than ever they have done in any former age, or in any other nation.[40]

Subject and Comment: **Modes of Faith a Personal Matter**

Washington: The liberty enjoyed by the people of these States, of worshipping Almighty God agreeably to their consciences, is not only among the choicest of their blessings, but also of their rights. While men perform their social duties faithfully, they do all that society or the state can with propriety demand or expect; and remain responsible only to their Maker for the religion, or modes of faith, which they may prefer or profess.

[39] Letter to United Baptist Church of Virginia, May, 1789.
[40] Letter to Episcopal Church, August 19, 1789.

Your principles and conduct are well known to
me; and it is doing the people call Quakers no
more than justice to say that (except their declining
to share with others the burthen [sic] of the common
defence) there is no denomination among us, who
are more exemplary and useful citizens.[41]

Subject and Comment: U.S. in Forefront of Justice and Liberality

Washington: I feel my conduct in War and in Peace
has met with more general approbation than could
reasonably have been expected; and I find myself
disposed to consider that fortunate circumstance,
and extraordinary candor of my fellow-citizens of
all denominations.

As mankind becomes more liberal, they will be
more apt to allow, that all those who conduct themselves as worthy members of the community are
equally entitled to the protection of civil government. I hope ever to see America among the fore-
most nations in examples of justice and liberality.
And I presume, that your fellow-citizens will not
forget the patriotic part which you took in the
accomplishment of their revolution, and the establishment of their government; or the important assistance, which they received, from a Nation in which
the Roman Catholic religion is professed. . . . May
the members of your Society in America, animated
alone by the pure spirit of Christianity, and still
conducting themselves as the faithful subject of
our free government, enjoy every temporal and
spiritual felicity.[42]

Subject and Comment: Everyman's Vine and Fig Tree

Washington: It would be consistent with the frankness
of my character not to avow that I am pleased
with your favorable opinion of my administration,
and fervent wishes for my felicity. May the Children
of the Stock of Abraham, who dwell in this land,

[41] Undated letter to Quakers.
[42] Letter to Roman Catholics, March 15, 1790.

continue to merit and enjoy the good will of the other inhabitants, while every one shall sit in safety under his own vine and fig-tree, and there shall be none to make him afraid. May the father of all mercies scatter light and not darkness in our paths, and make us all in our several vocations useful here, and in his own due time and way ever-lastingly happy.[43]

Subject and Comment: **Glorious Revolution and the Almighty**

Washington: The liberal sentiment towards each other which marks every political and religious denomination of men in this country stands unrivalled in the history of nations. The affection of such people is a treasure beyond the reach of calculation; and the repeated proofs which my fellow citizens have given of their attachment to me, and approbation of my doings form the purest source of my temporal felicity. The affectionate expressions of your address again excite my gratitude, and receive my warmest acknowledgments.

The power and goodness of the Almighty were strongly manifested in the events of our late glorious revolution, and his kind interposition in our behalf has been no less visible in the establishment of our present government. In war he directed the sword and in peace he has ruled in our councils, my agency in both has been guided by the best intentions, and a sense of the duty which I owe my country: and as my exertions hitherto have been amply rewarded by the approbation of my fellow-citizens, I shall endeavor to deserve a continuance of it by my future conduct. . . .[44]

Subject and Comment: **Truth Over Bigotry and Super-stition**

Washington: We have abundant reason to rejoice that in this Land the light of truth and reason

[43] Letter to Hebrew congregation of Newport, 1790.
[44] Letter to Hebrew congregation of Philadelphia, 1790.

has triumphed over the power of bigotry and superstition, and that every person may here worship
God according to the dictates of his own heart.
In this enlightened Age and in this Land of equal
liberty it is our boast, that a man's religious tenets
will not forfeit the protection of the Laws, nor
deprive him of the right of attaining and holding
the highest Offices that are known in the United
States.

Your prayers for my present and future felicity
are received with gratitude; and I sincerely wish,
Gentlemen, that you may in you social and individual
capacities taste those blessings, which a gracious
God bestows upon the Righteous.[45]

Subject and Comment: **Those Liberal Discourses**

Washington: To this public testimony of your approbation of my conduct and affection for my person
I am not insensible, and your prayers for my present
and future happiness merit my warmest acknowledgments. It is with peculiar satisfaction I can say
that, prompted by a high sense of duty in my attendance on public worship, I have been gratified,
during my residence among you , by the liberal
and interesting discourses which have been delivered
in your Churches.

Believing that that Government alone can be
approved by Heaven, which promotes peace and
secures protection to its Citizens in every thing
that is dear and interesting to them, it has been
the great object of my administration to insure
those invaluable ends; and when, to a consciousness
of the purity of intentions, is added the approbation
of my fellow Citizens, I shall experience in my
retirement that heartfelt satisfaction which can
only be exceeded by the hope of future happiness.[46]

Subject and Comment: **Dinner Bell and the Assessment**

Washington: I have this moment received yours

[45] Letter to a Baltimore church, January 27, 1793.

[46] Letter to Episcopal churches of Philadelphia, 1797.

of yesterday's date, enclosing a memorial and remonstrance against the Assessment Bill. . . .

Although, no man's sentiments are more opposed to any kind of restraint upon religious principles than mine are; yet I must confess that I am not amongst the number of those who are so much alarmed at the thoughts of making people pay towards the support of that which they profess, if of the denomination of Christians, or declare themselves Jews, Mohomitans or otherwise, and thereby obtain proper relief. As the matter now stands, I wish an assessment had never been agitated, and as it has gone so far, that the Bill could die an easy death; because I think it will be productive of more quiet to the State, than by enacting it into a Law; which, in my opinion, would be impolitic; admitting there is a decided majority for it, to the disquiet of a respectable minority. In the first case the matter will soon subside; in the latter, it will rankle and perhaps convulse, the State. The Dinner Bell rings, and I must conclude with an expression of my concern for your indisposition.[47]

Subject and Comment: **He Who Presides in the Councils of Nations**

Washington: It would be peculiarly improper to omit in this first official Act, my fervent supplications to that Almighty Being who rules over the Universe, who presides in the Councils of Nations, and whose providential aids can supply every human defect, that his benediction may consecrate to the liberties and happiness of the People of the United States, a Government instituted by themselves for these essential purposes: and may enable every instrument employed in its administration to execute with success, the functions allotted to his charge. In tendering this homage to the Great Author of every public and private good, I assure myself that it expresses your sentiments not less than my own; nor those of my fellow-citizens at large, less than either. No People can be bound to acknowledge and adore

[47] Letter to George Mason, October 3, 1785.

the invisible hand which conducts the Affairs of men more than the People of the United States. Every step, by which they have advanced to the character of an independent nation, seems to have been distinguished by some token of providential agency. And in the important revolution just accomplished in the system of their United Government, the tranquil deliberations and voluntary consent of so many distinct communities, from which the event has resulted, cannot be compared with the means by which most Governments have been established, without some return of pious gratitude along with humble anticipation of the future blessings which the past seem to presage. These reflections, arising out of the present crisis, have forced themselves too strongly on my mind to be suppressed. You will join me I trust in thinking that there are none under the influence of which, the proceedings of a new and free Government can more auspiciously commence.[48]

Subject and Comment: **Acrimony and Irreconcilable Hatreds**

Washington: I have now before me your letters of the 9 of January and 12 of February to which it will not be in my power to reply so fully as my inclination would lead me to do if I had no avocation but those of a personal nature.

I regret exceedingly that the disputes between the Protestants and Roman Catholics should be carried to the serious alarming height mentioned in your letters. Religious controversies are always productive of more acrimony and irreconcilable hatreds than those which spring from any other cause; and I was not without hopes that the enlightened and liberal policy of the present age would have put an effectual stop to contentions of this kind.[49]

Subject and Comment: **Great Republic of Humanity**

[48] Inagural address, April 30, 1789.
[49] Letter to Edward Newenham, June 22, 1792.

Washington: Although I pretend to no particular information respecting commercial affairs, nor any foresight into the scenes of futurity; yet as the member of an infant empire, as a philanthropist by character and (if I may be allowed the expression) as a citizen of the great republic of humanity at large; I cannot help turning my attention sometimes to this subject. I would be understood to mean, I cannot avoid reflecting with pleasure on the probable influence that commerce may hereafter have on human manners and society in general. On these occasions I consider how fond, perhaps an enthusiastic idea, that as the world is evidently much less barbarous than it has been, its melioration must still be progressive; that nations are becoming more humanized in their policy, that the subject of ambition and causes for hostility are daily diminishing, and, in fine, that the period is not very remote, when the benefits of a liberal and free commerce will, pretty generally, succeed to the devastations and horrors of war.[50]

Subject and Comment: **Reason and the Supreme Being**

Washington: It is impossible to account for the creation of the universe, without the agency of a Supreme Being.

It is impossible to govern the universe without the aid of a Supreme Being. It is impossible to reason without arriving at a Supreme Being. Religion is as necessary to reason, as reason is to religion. The one cannot exist without the other. A reasoning being would lose his reason, in attempting to account for the great phenomena of nature, had he not a Supreme Being to refer to; and well has it been said, that if there had been no God, mankind would have been obliged to imagine one.[51]

Subject and Comment: **Fellow Discipleship**

[50] Letter to Lafayette, August 15, 1786.
[51] Quotation attributed to Washington by Paulding.
See: Cousins, supra, pp. 72-73.

Adams: Ask me not, then, whether I am a Catholic or Protestant, Calvinist or Arminian. As far as they are Christian, I wish to be a fellow-disciple with them all.[52]

Subject and Comment: **Stupendous Plan and Astonishing Machine**

Adams: The minutest particle, in one of Saturn's satellites, may have some influence upon the most distant regions of the system. The stupendous plan of operation was projected by Him who rules the universe, and a part assigned to every particle of matter, to act in this great and complicated drama. The Creator looked into the remotest futurity, and saw his great designs accomplished by this inextricable, this mysterious complication of causes. But to rise still higher, this solar system is but one very small wheel in the great, the astonishing machine of the world. Those stars, that twinkle in the heavens, have each of them a choir of planets, comets, and satellites, dancing round them, playing mutually on each other, and all, together, playing on the other systems that lie around them.

Our system, considered as one body hanging on its center of gravity, may affect and be affected by all the other systems within the compass of creation. Thus it is highly probable every particle of matter influences and is influenced by every other particle in the whole collected universe.[53]

Subject and Comment: **Advantage of Christianity**

Adams: One great advantage of the Christian religion is that it brings the great principle of the law of nature and nations - Love your neighbor as yourself, and do to others as you would that others should do to you - to the knowledge, belief, and veneration of the whole people. Children, servants, women, and men, are all professors in the science of public and private morality. No other institution for education, no kind of political discipline, could

[52] Cousins, supra, p. 74.
[53] Adam's diary, May 1, 1756.

diffuse this kind of necessary information, so universally among all ranks and descriptions of citizens. The duties and rights of the man and the citizen are thus taught from early infancy to every creature. The Sanctions of a future life are thus added to the observance of civil and political, as well as domestic and private duties. Prudence, justice, temperance, and fortitude, are thus taught to be the means and conditions of future as well as present happiness.[54]

Subject and Comment: **Those Inevitable Evils of Life**

Adams: My religion is founded on the love of God and my neighbor; on the hope of pardon for my offences; upon contrition; upon the duty as well as the necessity of supporting with patience the inevitable evils of life; in the duty of doing no wrong, but all the good I can, to the creation, of which I am but an infinitesimal part. Are you a dissenter from this religion? I believe, too, in a future state of rewards and punishments, but not eternal.[55]

Subject and Comment: **Question God, Jesus, and Miracles. Avoid Servile Crouching.**

Jefferson: Religion. Your reason is now mature enough to examine this object. In the first place, divest yourself of all bias in favor of novelty and singularity of opinion. Indulge them in any other subject rather than that of religion. It is too important, and the consequences of error may be too serious. On the other hand, shake off all the fears and servile prejudices, under which weak minds are servilely crouched. Fix reason firmly in her seat, and call to her tribunal every fact, every opinion. Question with boldness even the existence of a God; because, if there be one, he must more approve of the homage of reason, than that of blindfolded fear.

[54] Adam's diary, August 14, 1796.
[55] Letter to F.A. Van der Kemp, July 13, 1815.

You will naturally examine first the religion of your own country. Read the Bible, then, as you would read Livy or Tacitus. The facts which are within the ordinary course of nature, you will believe on the authority of the writer, as you do those of the same kind in Livy and Tacitus. The testimony of the writer weighs in their favor, in one scale, and their not being against the laws of nature, does not weigh against them. But those facts in the Bible which contradict the laws of nature, must be examined with more care, and under a variety of faces. Here you must recur to the pretensions of the writer to inspiration from God. Examine upon what evidence his pretensions are founded, and whether that evidence is so strong, as that its falsehood would be more improbable than a change in the laws of nature, in the case he relates. For example, in the book of Joshua, we are told, the sun stood still several hours. Were we to read that fact in Livy or Tacitus, we should class it with their showers of blood, speaking of statues, beasts, etc. But it is said, that the writer of that book was inspired. Examine, therefore, candidly, what evidence there is of his having been inspired. The pretension is entitled to your inquiry, because millions believe it. On the other hand, you are astronomer enough to know how contrary it is to the law of nature that a body revolving on its axis, as the earth does, should have stopped, should not, by that sudden stoppage, have prostrated animals, trees, buildings, and should after a certain time have resumed its revolution, and that without a second general prostration. Is this arrest of the earth's motion, or the evidence which affirms it, most within the law of probabilities?

You will next read the New Testament. It is the history of a personage called Jesus. Keep in your eye the opposite pretensions: 1, of those who say he was begotten by God, born of a virgin, suspended and reversed the laws of nature at will, and ascended bodily into heaven; and 2, of those who say he was a man of illegitimate birth, of a benevolent heart, enthusiastic mind, who set out without pretensions to divinity, ended in believing them, and was punished capitally for sedition, by being gibbeted, according to the Roman law, which punished the first commission of that offense by whipping, and the second by exile, or death, in furea. See this law in the Digest, Lib. 48.tit.19. S28.3 and Lipsius Lib. 2 de cruce. cap. 2.

These questions are examined in the books I have mentioned, under the head of Religion, and several others. They will assist you in your inquiries; but keep your reason firmly on the watch in reading them all.

Do not be frightened from this inquiry by any fear of its consequences. If it ends in a belief that there is no God, you will find incitements to virtue in the comfort and pleasantness you feel in its exercise, and the love of others which it will procure you. If you find reason to believe there is a God, a consciousness that you are acting under his eye, and that he approves you, will be a vast additional incitement; if that there be a future state, the hope of a happy existence in that increases the appetite to deserve it; if that Jesus was also a God, you will be comforted by a belief of his aid and love.

In fine, I repeat, you must lay aside all prejudice on both sides, and neither believe nor reject any-thing because any other persons, or description of persons, have rejected it or believed it. Your own reason is the only oracle given you by heaven, and you are answerable, not for the rightness, but uprightness of the decision.

I forgot to observe, when speaking of the New Testament, that you should read all the histories of Christ, as well as those whom a council of ecclesiastics have decided for us, to be Pseudo-evangelists, as those they named Evangelists. Because these Pseudo-evangelists pretend to inspiration, as much as the others, and you are to judge their pretensions by your own reason, and not by the reason of those ecclesiastics. Most of these are lost. There are some, however, still extant, collected by Fabricius, which I will endeavor to get and send to you.[56]

[56] Letter to nephew Peter Carr, August 10, 1787.

Subject and Comment: **Dogma Supports Religious Teachers**

Jefferson: As to my self, my religious reading has long been confined to the moral branch of religion, which is the same in all religions; while in that branch which consists of dogmas, all differ, all have a different set. The former instructs us how to live well and worthily in society; the latter are made to interest our minds in the support of the teachers who inculcate them. Hence, for one sermon on a moral subject, you hear ten on the dogmas of the sect. However, religion is not the subject for you and me; neither of us know the religious opinions of the other; that is a matter between our Maker and ourselves. We understand each other better in politics, to which therefore I will proceed.[57]

Subject and Comment: **All Religions Agree**

Jefferson: Reading, reflection and time have convinced me that the interests of society require the observation of those moral precepts only in which all religions agree (for all forbid us to murder, steal, plunder, or bear false witness) and that we should not intermeddle with the particular dogmas in which all religions differ, and which are totally unconnected with morality.

In all of them we see good men, and as many in one as another. The varieties in the structure and action of the human mind as in those of the body, are the work of our creator, against which it cannot be a religious duty to erect the standard of uniformity. The practice of morality being necessary for the well-being of society, he has taken care to impress its precepts so indelibly on our hearts that they shall not be effaced by the subtleties of our brain. We all agree in the obligation of the moral precepts of Jesus, and nowhere will they be found delivered in greater purity than in his discourses.[58]

[57] Letter to Thomas Leiper, January 21, 1809.
[58] Letter to James Fishback, September 27, 1809.

Subject and Comment: **The Real Anti-Christ**

Jefferson: Nothing can be more exactly and seriously true than what is there stated; that but a short time elapsed after the death of the great reformer of the Jewish religion, before his principles were departed from by those who professed to be his special servants, and perverted into an engine for enslaving mankind, and aggrandizing their oppressors in Church and state; that the purest system of morals ever before preached to man has been adulterated and sophisticated by artificial constructions, into a mere contrivance to filch wealth and power to themselves; that rational men, not being able to swallow their impious heresies, in order to force them down their throats, they raise the hue and cry of infidelity, while themselves are the greatest obstacles to the advancement of the real doctrine of Jesus, and do, in fact, constitute the real Anti-Christ.[59]

Subject and Comment: **Don't Let Subtleties and Mysteries Confuse. All Good Men His Children.**

Jefferson: An eloquent preacher of your religious society, Richard Motte, in a discourse of much emotion and pathos, is said to have exclaimed aloud to his congregation, that he did not believe there was a Quaker, Presbyterian, Methodist, or Baptist in heaven, having paused to give his hearers time to stare and to wonder. He added, that in Heaven, God knew no distinctions, but considered all good men as his children, and as brethren of the same family.

I believe, with the Quaker preacher, that he who steadily observes those moral precepts in which all religions concur, will never be questioned at the gates of heaven, as to the dogmas in which they all differ. That on entering there, all these are left behind us, and the Aristides and Catos, and Penns and Tillotsons, Presbyterians and Baptists,

[59] Letter to Samuel Kercheral, January 19, 1810.

will find themselves united in all principles which are in concert with the reason of the supreme mind.

Of all the systems of morality, ancient or modern, which have come under my observation, none appear to me so pure as that of Jesus. He who follows this steadily need not, I think, be uneasy, although he cannot comprehend the subtleties and mysteries erected on his doctrines by those who, calling themselves his special followers and favorites, would make him come into the world to lay snares for all understandings but theirs.

These metaphysical heads, usurping the judgment seat of God, denounce as his enemies all who cannot perceive the Geometrical logic of Euclid in the demonstrations of St. Athanasius, that three are one, and one is three, and yet that one is not three nor the three one.[60]

Subject and Comment: **No Denominations In Heaven**

Jefferson: Our particular principles of religion are a subject of accountability to our God alone. I inquire after no man's, and trouble none with mine; nor is it given to us in this life to know whether yours or mine, our friends or our foes, are exactly the right. Nay, we have heard it said that there is not a Quaker or a Baptist, a Presbyterian or an Episcopalian, a Catholic or a Protestant in heaven; that on entering that gate, we leave those badges of schism behind, and find ourselves united in those principles only in which God has united us all. Let us not be uneasy then about the different roads we may pursue, as believing them the shortest, to that our last abode; but, following the guidance of a good conscience, let us be happy in the hope that by these different paths we shall all meet in the end. And that you and I, may there meet and embrace, is my earnest prayer.[61]

Subject and Comment: **Jefferson's New Testament. Watch Out for Plato.**

[60] Letter to William Canby, September 18, 1813.
[61] Letter to Miles King, September 26, 1814.

Jefferson: I, too, have made a wee-little book from the same materials, which I call the Philosophy of Jesus; it is a paradigma of his doctrines, made by cutting the texts out of the book and arranging them on the pages of a blank book, in a certain order of time or subject. A more beautiful or precious morsel of ethics I have never seen; it is a document in proof that I am a real Christian, that is to say, a disciple of the doctrines of Jesus, very different from the Platonists, who call me infidel and themselves Christians and preachers of the gospel, while they draw all their characteristic dogmas from what its author never said nor saw. They have compounded from the heathen mysteries a system beyond the comprehension of man, of which the great reformer of the vicious ethics and deism of the Jews, were he to return to earth, would not recognize one feature.[62]

Subject and Comment: **Crazy Theologists and Those Who Call Themselves His Ministers**

Jefferson: We probably differ on the dogmas of theology, the foundation of all sectarianism, and on which no two sects dream alike; for if they did they would then be of the same. You say you are a Calvinist. I am not. I am of a sect by myself, as far as I know. I am not a Jew, and therefore do not adopt their theology, which supposes the God of infinite justice to punish the sins of the fathers upon their children, unto the third and fourth generations; and the benevolent and sublime reformer of that religion has told us only that God is good and perfect, but has not defined him.

I am, therefore, of his theology, believing that we have neither words nor ideas adequate to that definition. And if we could all, after this example, leave the subject as undefinable, we should all be of one sect, doers of good, and eschewers of evil. No doctrines of his lead to schism. It is the speculations of crazy theologists which have made a Babel

[62]Letter to Charles Thomson, January 9, 1816.

of a religion the most moral and sublime ever preached to man, and calculated to heal, and not to
create differences. These religious animosities I
impute to those who call themselves his ministers,
and who engraft their casuistries on the stock of
his simple precepts. I am sometimes more angry
with them than is authorized by the blessed charities which he preaches.[63]

Subject and Comment: **A Counterpoise of Good
Works Separates Gold from Dross**

Jefferson: But while this syllabus is meant to place
the character of Jesus in its true and high light,
as no impostor himself, but a great reformer of
the Hebrew code of religion, it is not to be understood that I am with him in all his doctrines. I
am a Materialist; he takes the side of Spiritualism;
he preaches the efficacy of repentance towards
forgiveness of sin; I require a counterpoise of good
works to redeem it, etc., etc. It is the innocence
of his character, the purity and sublimity of his
moral precepts, the eloquence of his inculcations,
the beauty of the apologues in which he conveys
them, that I so much admire; sometimes, indeed,
needing indulgence to eastern hyperbolism. My eulo-
gies, too, may be founded on a postulate which
all may not be ready to grant. Among the sayings
and discourses imputed to him by his biographers,
I find many passages of fine imagination, correct
morality, and of the most lovely benevolence; and
others, again, of so much ignorance, so much absurd-
ity, so much untruth, charlatanism and imposture,
as to pronounce it impossible that such contradictions should have proceeded from the same being.
I separate, therefore, the gold from the dross; restore
to him the former, and leave the latter to the
stupidity of some, and roguery of others of his
disciples. Of this band of dupes and imposters, Paul
was the great Coryphaeus, and first corruptor of
the doctrines of Jesus. These palpable interpolations and falsifications of his doctrines, led me
to try to sift them apart. I found the work obvious

[63] Letter to Ezra Stiles, June 25, 1819.

and easy, and that his part composed the most beautiful morsel of morality which has been given to us by man. The syllabus is therefore of his doctrines, not all of mine. I read them as I do those of other ancient and modern moralists, with a mixture of approbation and dissent.[64] . . .

Subject and Comment: **Sweating Blood and Thinking for Ourselves**

Jefferson: For if we could believe that he really countenanced the follies, the falsehoods, and the charlatanisms which his biographers father on him, and admit the misconstructions, interpolations, and theorizations of the fathers of the early, and fanatics of the latter ages, the conclusion would be irresistible by every sound mind, that he was an impostor. I give no credit to their falsifications of his actions and doctrines, and to rescue his character, the postulate in my letter asked only what is granted in reading every other historian. When Livy and Siculus, for example, tell us things which coincide with our experience of the order of nature, we credit them on their word, and place their narrations among the records of credible history. But when they tell us of calves speaking, of statues sweating blood, and other things against the course of nature, we reject these as fables not belonging to history. In like manner, when an historian, speaking of a character well known and established on satisfactory testimony, imputes to it things incompatible with that character, we reject them without hesitation, and assent to that only of which we have better evidence. Had Plutarch informed us that Caesar and Cicero passed their whole lives in religious exercises, and abstinence from the affairs of the world, we should reject what was so inconsistent with their established characters, still crediting what he relates in conformity with our ideas of them.

* * *

But Plato's visions have furnished a basis for endless systems of mystical theology, and he is therefore

[64] Letter to William Short, April 13, 1820, re. Jefferson's plans to re-write the New Testament.

all but adopted as a Christian saint. It is surely time for men to think for themselves, and to throw off the authority of names so artificially magnified. . . . I say, that his free exercise of reason is all I ask for the vindication of the character of Jesus. We find in the writings of his biographers matter of two distinct descriptions. First, a groundwork of vulgar ignorance, of things impossible, of superstitions, fanaticisms, and fabrications. Intermixed with these, again, are sublime ideas of the Supreme Being, aphorisms, and precepts of the purest morality and benevolence, sanctioned by a life of humility, innocence and simplicity of manners, neglect of riches, absence of worldly ambition and honors, with an eloquence and persuasiveness which have not been surpassed. These could not be inventions of the grovelling authors who relate to them. They are far beyond the powers of their feeble minds. They show that there was a character, the subject of their history, whose splendid conceptions were above all suspicion of being interpolations from their hands. Can we be at a loss in separating such materials, and ascribing each to its genuine author? The difference is obvious to the eye and to the understanding, and we may read as we run to each his part; and I will venture to affirm, that he who, as I have done, will undertake to winnow this grain from the chaff, will find it not to require a moment's consideration. The parts fall asunder of themselves, as would those of an image of metal and clay.

There are, I acknowledge, passages not free from objection, which we may, with probability, ascribe to Jesus himself; but claiming indulgence from the circumstances under which he acted. His object was the reformation of some articles in the religion of the Jews, as taught by Moses. That sect had presented for the object of their worship, a being of terrific character, cruel, vindictive, capricious, and unjust. Jesus, taking for his type the best qualities of the human head and heart, wisdom, justice, goodness, and adding to them power, ascribed all of these, but in infinite perfection, to the Supreme Being, and formed him

really worthy of their adoration. Moses had either
not believed in a future state of existence, or
had not thought it essential to be explicitly taught
to his people. Jesus inculcated that doctrine with
emphasis and precision. Moses had bound the Jews
to many idle ceremonies, mummeries, and obser-
vances of no effect towards producing the social
utilities which constitute the essence of virtue;
Jesus exposed their futility and insignificance. The
one instilled into his people the most anti-social
spirit toward other nations; the other preached
philanthropy and universal charity and benevolence.
The office of reformer of the superstitions of a
nation, is ever dangerous. Jesus had to walk on
the perilous confines of reason and religion; and
a step to right or left might place him within the
grasp of the priests of the superstition, a blood-
thirsty race, as cruel and remorseless as the being
whom they represented as the family God of
Abraham, of Isaac and of Jacob, and the local God
of Israel. They were constantly laying snares, too,
to entangle him in the web of the law. He was
justifiable, therefore, in avoiding these by evasions,
by sophisms, by misconstructions and misapplications
of scraps of the prophets, and in defending himself
with these their own weapons, as sufficient, ad
homines, at least. That Jesus did not mean to impose
himself on mankind as the son of God, physically
speaking, I have been convinced by the writings
of men more learned than myself in that lore. But
that he might conscientiously believe himself inspired
from above, is very possible. The whole religion
of the Jew, inculcated on him from his infancy,
was founded in the belief of divine inspiration.
The fumes of the most disorded [sic] imaginations
were recorded in their religious code, as special
communications of the Deity; and as it could not
but happen that in the course of ages, events would
now and then turn up to which some of these vague
rhapsodies might be accommodated by the aid of
allegories, figures, types, and other tricks upon
words, they have not only preserved their credit
with the Jews of all subsequent times, but are
the foundation of much of the religions of those

who have schismatized from them. Elevated by the enthusiasm of a warm and pure heart, conscious of the high strains of an eloquence which had not been taught him, he might readily mistake the coruscations of his own fine genius for inspirations of an higher order. This belief carried, therefore, no more personal imputation, than the belief of Socrates, that himself was under the care and admonitions of a guardian Daemon. And how many of our wisest men still believe in the reality of these inspirations, while perfectly sane on all other subjects. Excusing, therefore, on these considerations, those passages in the gospels which seem to bear marks of weakness in Jesus, ascribing to him what alone is consistent with the great and pure character of which the same writings furnish proofs, and to their proper authors their own trivialities and imbecilities, I think myself authorized to conclude the purity and distinction of his character, in opposition to the impostures which those authors would fix upon him; and that the postulate of my former letter is no more than is granted in all other historical works.[65]

Subject and Comment: **Polytheism and the Genuine Jesus**

Jefferson: I hold the precepts of Jesus, as delivered by himself, to be the most pure, benevolent, and sublime, which have ever been preached to man. I adhere to the principles of the first age; and consider all subsequent innovations as corruptions of this religion, having no foundation in what came from him. The metaphysical insanities of Athanasius, of Loyola, and of Calvin, are, to my understanding, mere re-lapses into polytheism, differing from paganism only by being more unintelligible. The religion of Jesus is founded in the unity of God, and this principle, chiefly, gave it triumph over the rabble of heathen gods then acknowledged. Thinking men of all nations rallied readily to the doctrine of one only God, and embraced it with the pure morals which Jesus inculcated. If the

[65] Letter to William Short, August 4, 1820.

freedom of religion, guaranteed to us by law in theory, can ever rise in practice under the overbearing inquisition of public opinion, truth will prevail over fanaticism, and the genuine doctrines of Jesus, so long perverted by his pseudopriests, will again be restored to their original purity. This reformation will advance with the other improvements of the human mind, but too late for me to witness it.[66]

Subject and Comment: **Trinitarian Arithmetic. Mysteries, Fancies, and Falsehoods.**

Jefferson: When we shall have done away the incomprehensible jargon of the Trinitarian arithmetic, that three are one, and one is three; when we shall have knocked down the artificial scaffolding, reared to mask from view the simple structure of Jesus; when, in short, we shall have unlearned everything which has been taught since his day, and got back to the pure and simple doctrines he inculcated, we shall then be truly and worthily his disciples; and my opinion is that if nothing had ever been added to what flowed purely from his lips, the whole world would at this day have been Christian. I know that the case you cite, of Dr. Drake, has been a common one. The religion-builders have so distorted and deformed the doctrines of Jesus, so muffled them in mysticisms, fancies and falsehoods, have caricatured them into forms so monstrous and inconceivable as to shock reasonable thinkers, to revolt them against the whole, and drive them rashly to pronounce its founder an impostor. Had there never been a commentator, there never would have been an infidel. In the present advance of truth, which we both approve, I do not know that you and I may think alike on all points. As the Creator has made no two faces alike, so no two minds, and probably no two creeds.[67]

Subject and Comment: **One Body, Three Heads**

Jefferson: I have to thank you for pamphlets on

[66] Letter to Jared Sparks, November 4, 1820.
[67] Letter to Timothy Pikering, February 27, 1821.

the subject of Unitarianism, and to express my gratification with your efforts for the revival of primitive Christianity in your quarter. No historical fact is better established, than that the doctrine of one God, pure and uncompounded, was that of the early ages of Christianity; and was among the efficacious doctrines which gave it triumph over the polytheism of the ancients, sickened with the absurdities of their own theology. Nor was the unity of the Supreme Being ousted from the Christian creed by the force of reason, but by the sword of civil government, wielded at the will of the fanatic Athanasius. The hocus-pocus phantasm of a God like another Cerberus, with one body and three heads, had its birth and growth in the blood of thousands and thousands of martyrs. And a strong proof of the solidity of the primitive faith, is its restoration, as soon as a nation arises which vindicates to itself the freedom of religious opinion, and its external divorce from the civil authority. The pure and simple unity of the Creator of the universe, is now all but ascendant in the eastern States; it is dawning in the West, and advancing towards the South; and I confidently expect that the present generation will see Unitarianism become the general religion of the United States. The Eastern presses are giving us many excellent pieces on the subject, and Priestley's learned writings on it are, or should be, in every hand. In fact, the Athanasian paradox that one is three, and three but one, is so incomprehensible to the human mind, that no candid man can say he has any idea of it, and how can he believe what presents no idea? He who thinks he does, only deceives himself. He proves, also, that man, once surrendering his reason, has no remaining guard against absurdities the most monstrous, and like a ship without a rudder is the sport of every wind. With such persons, gullibility, which they call faith, takes the helm from the hand of reason, and the mind becomes a wreck.[68]

Subject and Comment: **Happiness in Pure Jesus**

[68] Letter to James Smith, December 8, 1822.

Jefferson: The doctrines of Jesus are simple, and tend all to the happiness of man.

1. That there is one only God, and he all perfect.

2. That to love God with all thy heart and thy neighbor as thyself is the sum of religion. These are the great points on which he endeavored to reform the religion of the Jews. But compare with these the demoralizing dogmas of Calvin.

1. That there are three Gods.

2. That good works, or the love of our neighbor, are nothing.

3. That faith is everything, and the more incomprehensible the proposition, the more merit in its faith.

4. That reason in religion is of unlawful use.

5. That God, from the beginning, elected certain individuals to be saved, and certain others to be damned; and that no crimes of the former can damn them; no virtues of the latter save.

* * *

But much I fear, that when this great truth shall be re-established, its votaries will fall into the fatal error of fabricating formulas of creed and confessions of faith, the engines which so soon destroyed the religion of Jesus, and made of Christendom a mere Aceldama; that they will give up morals for mysteries, and Jesus for Plato. How much wiser are the Quakers, who, agreeing in the fundamental doctrines of the gospel, schismatize about no mysteries, and, keeping within the pale of common sense, suffer no speculative differences of opinion, any more than of feature, to impair the love of their brethren. Be this the wisdom of Unitarians, this the holy mantle which shall cover within its charitable circumference all who believe in one God, and who love their neighbor! [69]

Subject and Comment: **Don't You Just Love Jesus?**

Jefferson: In our Richmond there is much fanaticism, but chiefly among the women. They have their night meetings and praying parties, where, attended

[69] Letter to Benjamin Waterhouse, June 26, 1822.

by their priests, and sometimes by a hen-pecked
husband, they pour forth the effusions of their love
of Jesus, in terms as amatory and carnal, as their
modesty would permit them to use to a mere earthly
lover.[70]

Subject and Comment: **Authors of New Testament**

Jefferson: To do him [Jesus] justice, it would be
necessary to remark the disadvantages his doctrines
had to encounter, not having been committed to
writing by himself, but by the most unlettered of
men, by memory, long after they had heard them
from him; when much was forgotten, much misunderstood, and presented in every paradoxical shape.[71]

Subject and Comment: **Love Humankind, Not Just
Kindred and Friends. Words of Jesus.**

Jefferson: Let a just view be taken of the moral
principles inculcated by the most esteemed of the
sects of ancient philosophy, or of their individuals;
particularly Pythagoras, Socrates, Epicurus, Cicero,
Epictetus, Seneca, Antoninus.
I. Philosophers. 1. Their precepts related chiefly
to ourselves, and the government of those passions
which, unrestrained, would disturb our tranquility
of mind. In this branch of philosophy they were
really great. 2. In developing our duties to others,
they were short and defective. They embraced,
indeed, the circles of kindred and friends and inculcated patriotism, or the love of our country in
the aggregate, as a primary obligation; towards
our neighbors and countrymen they taught justice,
but scarcely viewed them as within the circle of
benevolence. Still less have they inculcated peace,
charity, and love to our fellow men, or embraced
with benevolence the whole of mankind.
II. Jews. 1. Their system was Deism; that is,
the belief in one only God. But their ideas of him
and his attributes were degrading and injurious.
2. Their Ethics were not only imperfect, but often

[70] Letter to Thomas Cooper, November 2, 1822.
[71] Letter to Joseph Priestly, April 9, 1803.

irreconcilable with the sound dictates of reason and morality, as they respect intercourse with those around us; and repulsive and anti-social, as respecting other nations. They needed reformation, therefore, in an eminent degree.

III. Jesus. In this state of things among the Jews, Jesus appeared. His parentage was obscure; his condition poor; his education null; his natural endowments great; his life correct and innocent; he was meek, benevolent, patient, firm, disinterested, and of the sublimest eloquence.

The disadvantages under which his doctrines appear are remarkable.

1. Like Socrates and Epictetus, he wrote nothing himself.

2. But he had not, like them, a Xenophon or an Arrian to write for him. I name not Plato, who only used the name of Socrates to cover the whimsies of his own brain. On the contrary, all the learned of his country, entrenched in its power and riches, were opposed to him, lest his labors should undermine their advantages; and the committing to writing his life and doctrines fell on unlettered and ignorant men; who wrote, too, from memory, and not till long after the transactions had passed.

3. According to the ordinary fate of those who attempt to enlighten and reform mankind, he fell an early victim to the jealousy and combination of the altar and the throne, at about thirty-three years of age, his reason having not yet attained the maximum of its energy, nor the course of his preaching, which was but of three years at most, presented occasions for developing a complete system of morals.

4. Hence, the doctrines which he really delivered were defective as a whole, and fragments only of what he did deliver have come to us mutilated, misstated, and often unintelligible.

5. They have been still more disfigured by the corruptions of schismatising followers, who have found an interest in sophisticating and perverting the simple doctrines he taught, by engrafting on them the mysticisms of a Grecian sophist, frittering them into subtleties, and obscuring them with jargon,

until they have caused good men to reject the whole in disgust and to view Jesus himself as an imposter.

Notwithstanding these disadvantages, a system of morals is presented to us which, if filled up in the style and spirit of the rich fragments he left us, would be the most perfect and sublime that has ever been taught by man.

He [Jesus] corrected the Deism of the Jews, confirming them in their belief of one only God, and giving them juster notions of his attributes and government.

His moral doctrines, relating to kindred and friends, were more pure and perfect than those of the most correct of the philosophers, and greatly more so than those of the Jews; and they went far beyond both in inculcating universal philantropy, not only to kindred and friends, to neighbors and countrymen, but to all mankind, gathering all into one family, under the bonds of love, charity, peace, common wants, and common aids. A development of this head will evince the peculiar superiority of the system of Jesus over all others.

The precepts of philosophy, and of the Hebrew code, laid hold of actions only. He pushed his scrutinies into the heart of man; erected his tribunal in the region of his thoughts, and purifies the waters at the fountain head.

He taught, emphatically, the doctrines of a future state, which was either doubted, or disbelieved by the Jews; and wielded it with efficacy, as an important incentive, supplementary to the other motives to moral conduct.[72]

Subject and Comment: **Jugglers and Moneymakers**

Jefferson: To this Syllabus and extract, if a history of his life can be added, written with the same view of the subject, the world will see, after the fogs shall be dispelled, in which for fourteen centuries he has been enveloped by jugglers to make money of him, when the genuine character shall be exhibited, which they have dressed up in the rags of an imposter, the world, I say, will at length

[72] Re. Jefferson's re-write of the New Testament. See: Cousins, supra, pp. 169-171.

see the immortal merit of this first of human sages.

* * *

Nor can it be a work of labor, or of volume, for his journeyings from Judea to Samaria, and Samaria to Galilee, do not cover much country; and the incidents of his life require little research. They are all at hand, and need only to be put into human dress; noticing such only as are within the physical laws of nature, and offending none by a denial or even a mention of what is not.[73]

Subject and Comment: **Getting to Heaven**

Adams: He who loves the workman and his work, and does what he can to preserve it shall be accepted of him.[74]

Subject and Comment: **The Word of God?**

Adams: Aristotle wrote the history of eighteen hundred republics which existed before his time. Cicero wrote two volumes of discourses on government, which, perhaps, were worth all the rest of his works. The works of Livy and Tacitus, &c., that are lost, would be more interesting than all that remain. Fifty gospels have been destroyed, and where are St. Luke's world of books that have been written? If you ask my opinion who has committed all the havoc, I will answer you candidly, - Ecclesiastical and Imperial despotism has done it, to conceal their frauds.[75]

Subject and Comment: **Howl, Snarl and Bite. Fright Does Not Make Right.**

[73] Letter to F.A. Van der Kemp, April 25, 1816.
[74] Letter to Thomas Jefferson, June 28, 1830.
[75] Letter to Thomas Jefferson, July 9, 1813.

Adams: The human understanding is a revelation from its Maker, which can never be disputed or doubted. There can be no scepticism, Pyrrhonism, or incredulity or infidelity, here. No prophecies, no miracles are necessary to prove this celestial communication. The revelation has made it certain that two and one make three, and that one is not three nor can three be one. We can never be so certain of any prophecy, or the fulfilment of any prophecy, or of any miracle, or the design of any miracle, as we are from the revelation of nature, that is, Nature's God, that two and two are equal to four. Miracles or prophecies might frighten us out of our wits: might scare us to death; might induce us to lie, to say that we believe that two and two make five. But we should not believe it. We should know the contrary.

Had you and I been forty days with Moses on Mount Sinai, and admitted to behold the divine Shekinah, and there told that one was three and three one, we might not have had courage to deny it, but we could not have believed it. The thunders and lightnings, and earthquakes, and the transcendent splendors and glories might have overwhelmed us with terror and amazement, but we could not have believed the doctrine.

*   *   *

He created the universe. His duration is eternal, a parte ante and a parte post. His presence is as extensive as space. What is space? An infinite spherical vacuum. He created this speck of dirt and the human species for his glory, and with the deliberate design of making nine-tenths of our species miserable, forever, for his glory. This is the doctrine of Christian Theologians, in general, ten to one. Now, my friend, can prophecies or miracles convince you or me that infinite benevolence, wisdom and power, created, and preserved for a time, innumerable millions, to make them miserable forever, for his own glory? Wretch! What is his glory? Is he ambitious? Does he want promotion? Is he vain, tickled with adulation, exulting and triumphing in his power and the sweetness of his vengeance? Pardon me, my Maker, for these awful questions. My answer to them is always ready. I believe no such things. My adoration of the Author of the Universe is too profound and too sincere. The love of God and his creation - delight, joy, triumph, exultation in my own existence - though but an atom, a molecule organique in the universe - are my religion.

Howl, snarl, bite, ye Calvinistic, ye Athanasian divines, if you will. Ye will say I am no Christian. I say ye are no Christians, and there the account is balanced. Yet I believe all the honest men among you are Christians, in my sense of the word.[76]

Subject and Comment: **Transvestied Instruments of Riches**

Jefferson: In extracting the pure principles which he taught, we should have to strip off the artificial vestments in which they have been muffled by priests, who have travestied them into various forms, as instruments of riches and power to themselves. We must dismiss the Platonists and Plotinists, the Stagyrites and Gamalielites, the Eclectics, the Gnostics and Scholastics, their essences and emanations, their Logos and Demiurgos, Aeons and Daemons, male and female, with a long train of etc., etc., etc., or, shall I say at once, of nonsense. We must reduce our volume to the simple evangelists, select, even from them, the very words only of Jesus, paring off the amphiboligisms into which they have been led, by forgetting often, or not understanding, what had fallen from him, by giving their own misconceptions as his dicta, and expressing unintelligibly for others what they had not understood themselves. There will be found remaining the most sublime and benevolent code of morals which has ever been offered to man.

I have performed this operation for my own use, by cutting verse by verse out of the printed book, and arranging the matter which is evidently his, and which is as easily distinguishable as diamonds

[76] Letter to Thomas Jefferson, September 14, 1813.

in a dunghill. The result is an octavo of forty-six pages, of pure and unsophisticated doctrines, such as were professed and acted on by the unlettered Apostles, the Apostolic Fathers, and the Christians of the first century. Their Platonizing successors, indeed, in after times, in order to legitimate the corruptions which they had incorporated into the doctrines of Jesus, found it necessary to disavow the primitive Christians, who had taken their principles from the mouth of Jesus himself, of his Apostles, and the Fathers contemporary with them. They excommunicated their followers as heretics, branding them with the opprobrious name of Ebionites or Beggars.[77]

Subject and Comment: **Shocking Morality**

Adams: The Psalms of David, in sublimity, beauty, pathos, and originality, or, in one word, in poetry, are superior to all the odes, hymns and songs in our language. But I had rather read them in our prose translation than in any version I have seen. His morality, however, often shocks me, like Tristram Shandy's execrations.[78]

Subject and Comment: **Best Book in the World**

Adams: Philosophy is not only the love of wisdom, but the science of the universe and its cause. There is, there was, and there will be but one master of philosophy in the universe. Portions of it, in different degrees, are revealed to creatures. Philosophy looks with an impartial eye on all terrestrial religions. I have examined all, as well as my narrow sphere, my straitened means, and my busy life would allow me; and the result is, that the Bible is the best book in the world.[79]

Subject and Comment: **The Fall of Man Allegory**

[77] Letter to John Adams, October 13, 1813.
[78] Letter to Thomas Jefferson, November 15, 1813.
[79] Letter to Thomas Jefferson, December 25, 1813.

Adams: [Quoting Priestly] "There is no circumstance of which Dr. Dupuis avails himself so much, or repeats so often, both with respect to the Jewish and Christian religions, as the history of the Fall of Man, in the book of Genesis." I believe with him, and have maintained in my writings, that this history is either an allegory, or founded on uncertain tradition, that it is an hypothesis to account for the facts.[80]

Subject and Comment: **King James Version**

Adams: We have now, it seems, a national Bible Society, to propagate King James's Bible through all nations. Would it not be better to apply these pious subscriptions to purify Christendom from the corruptions of Christianity than to propagate those corruptions in Europe, in Asia, Africa, and America? Suppose we should project a society to translate Dupuis into all languages and offer a reward in medals of diamonds to any man or body of men who would produce the best answer to it. . . .

Conclude not from all this that I have renounced the Christian religion, or that I agree with Dupuis in all his sentiments. Far from it. I see in every page something to recommend Christianity in its purity, and something to discredit its corruptions. If I had strength, I would give you my opinion of it in a fable of the bees. The Ten Commandments and the Sermon on the Mount contain my religion.

I agree perfectly with you that "moral sense is as much a part of our condition as that of feeling," and in all that you say upon his subject.[81]

Subject and Comment: **Unknown Essence**

Adams: When we say God is a spirit, we know what we mean, as well as we do when we say that the pyramids of Egypt are matter. Let us be content, therefore, to believe him to be a spirit, that is, an essence that we know nothing of, in which origin-

[80] Letter to Thomas Jefferson, February of 1814.
[81] Letter to Thomas Jefferson, November 4, 1816.

ally and necessarily reside all energy, all power, all capacity, all activity, all wisdom, all goodness.

Behold the creed and confession of faith of your ever affectionate friend.[82]

Subject and Comment: **God, Not Jesus, Created Universe**

Jefferson: I hold (without appeal to revelation) that when we take a view of the universe, in its parts, general or particular, it is impossible for the human mind not to perceive and feel a conviction of design, consummate skill, and indefinite power in every atom of its composition. The movements of the heavenly bodies, so exactly held in their course by the balance of centrifugal and centripetal forces; the structure of our earth itself, with its distribution of lands, waters and atmosphere; animal and vegetable bodies, examined in all their minutest particles; insects, mere atoms of life, yet as perfectly organized as man or mammouth; the mineral substances, their generation and uses; it is impossible, I say, for the human mind not to believe, that there is in all this, design, cause and effect, up to an ultimate cause, a fabricator of all things from matter and motion, their preserver and regulator while permitted to exist in their present forms, and their regeneration into new and other forms.

We see, too, evident proofs of the necessity of a superintending power, to maintain the universe in its course and order. Stars, well known, have disappeared, new ones have come into view; comets, in their incalculable courses, may run foul of suns and planets, and require renovation under other laws; certain races of animals are become extinct; and were there no restoring power, all existences might extinguish successively, one by one, until all should be reduced to a shapeless chaos. So irresistible are these evidences of an intelligent and powerful agent, that, of the infinite numbers of men who have existed through all time, they have believed, in the proportion of a million at least

[82]Letter to Thomas Jefferson, January 17, 1820.

to unit, in the hypothesis of an eternal pre-existence of a creator, rather than in that of a self-existent universe. Surely this unanimous sentiment renders this more probable, than that of the few in the other hypothesis. Some early Christians, indeed, have believed in the co-eternal pre-existence of both the creator and the world, without changing their relation of cause and effect. . . .
Of the nature of this being we know nothing. Jesus tells us, that "God is a spirit." John 4:24. But without defining what a spirit is. . . . Down to the third century, we know it was still deemed material; but of a lighter, subtler matter than our gross bodies. So says Origen. . . . So also Tertullian. . . . These two fathers were of the third century. Calvin's character of this Supreme Being seems chiefly copied from that of the Jews. But the reformation of these blasphemous attributes, and substitution of those more worthy, pure and sublime, seems to have been the chief object of Jesus in his discourses to the Jews; and his doctrine of the cosmogony of the world is very clearly laid down in the first three verses of the first chapter of John. . . . Which truly translated means, "In the beginning God existed, and reason [or mind] was with God, and that mind was God. This was in the beginning with God. All things were created by it, and without it was made not one thing which was made."

Yet this text, so plainly declaring the doctrine of Jesus, that the world was created by the supreme, intelligent being, has been perverted by modern Christians to build up a second person of their tritheism, by a mistranslation of the word λόγος. One of its legitimate meanings, indeed, is "a word." But in that sense it makes an unmeaning jargon; while the other meaning "reason," equally legitimate, explains rationally the eternal pre-existence of God, and his creation of the world.

Knowing how incomprehensible it was that "a word," the mere action or articulation of the organs of speech could create a world, they undertook to make of this articulation a second pre-existing being, and ascribe to him, and not to God, the creation of the universe. The atheist here plumes himself on the uselessness of such a God, and the simpler hypothesis of a self-existent universe.

The truth is, that the greatest enemies of the doctrines of Jesus are those, calling themselves the expositors of them, who have perverted them for the structure of a system of fancy absolutely incomprehensible, and without any foundation in his genuine words. And the day will come, when the mystical generation of Jesus, by the Supreme Being as his father, in the womb of a virgin, will be classed with the fable of the generation of Minerva in the brain of Jupiter. But we may hope that the dawn of reason and freedom of thought in these United States, will do away all this artificial scaffolding and restore to us the primitive and genuine doctrines of this the most venerated reformer of human errors.

So much for your quotation of Calvin's "mon Dieu! jusqu'a quand!" in which, when addressed to the God of Jesus, and our God, I join you cordially, and await his time and will with more readiness than reluctance. May we meet there again, in Congress, with our ancient colleagues, and receive with them the seal of approbation, "well done, good and faithful servants."[83]

Subject and Comment: **Which Word is The Word**

Madison: What edition; Hebrew, Septuagint, or Vulgate? What copy, what translation?

What books canonical, what apocryphal? the papists hold to be the former what protestants the latter, the Lutherans the latter what the protestants ye former.

In what light are they to be viewed, as dictated every letter by inspiration, or the essential parts only? Or matter in general not the words?[84]

[ALEXANDER HAMILTON: Writer of pamphlets supporting revolution against Great Britain. Aid to Washington. Supported limited but adequate

[83] Letter to John Adams, April 11, 1823.
[84] Re. Bible from notes on speech. November of 1784.

federal government at the Constitutional Convention.
One of the issuers of The Federalist papers. At
one time considered the possibility of a "Christian
Constitutional Society." First Secretary of the Treasury.]

Subject and Comment: **Liberty Greatest Blessing**

Hamilton: I am inviolably attached to the essential
rights of mankind, and the true interests of society.
I consider liberty in a genuine unadulterated sense,
as the greatest of terrestrial blessings. I am convinced that the whole human race is entitled to it,
and that it can be wrested from no part of them,
without the blackest and most aggravated guilt.[85]

Subject and Comment: **God As Comforter**

Hamilton: I need not tell you of the pangs I feel
from the idea of quitting you and exposing you
to the anguish I know you would feel. . . . The
consolations of religion, my beloved, can alone support you; and these you have a right to enjoy. Fly
to the bosom of your God, and be comforted.[86]

Subject and Comment: **Vile Worm and Idle Alarms**

Hamilton: My reflections and feelings on this frightful and melancholy occasion, are set forth in the
following self-discourse.
    Where now, oh! vile worm, is all thy boasted
fortitude and resolution? what is become of thy
arrogance and self-sufficiency? - why dost thou
tremble and stand aghast? how humble - how helpless - how contemptible you now appear. And for
why? the jarring elements - the discords of clouds?
Oh, impotent presumptuous fool! how durst thou
offend that Omnipotence whose nod alone were
sufficient to quell the destruction that hovers over
thee, or crush thee into atoms? see thy wretched
helpless state, and learn to know thyself. Learn
to know the best support. Despise thyself, and adore

[85] See: Cousins, supra, p. 326.
[86] Letter to his wife before duelling with Aaron Burr. See:
Cousins, supra, p. 329.

thy God. How sweet - how unutterably sweet were now, the voice of an approving conscience. Then couldst thou say - hence ye idle alarms, why do I shrink? what have I to fear? a pleasing calm suspense! a short repose from calamity to end in eternal bliss? Let the Earth rend - let the planets forsake their course - let the Sun be extinguished and the Heavens burst asunder - yet what have I to dread? my staff can never be broken - in Omnipotence I trusted. . . .[87]

Subject and Comment: **Succor the Miserable**

Hamilton: Yet, hold, Oh vain mortal! - check thy ill timed joy. Art thou so selfish to exult because thy lot is happy in a season of universal woe? Hast thou no feeling for the miseries of thy fellow-creatures? and art thou incapable of the soft pangs of sympathetic sorrow? - Look around thee and shudder at the view. See desolation and ruin where'er thou turnest thine eye?. . . Hark the bitter groans of distress. . . Oh distress unspeakable! my heart bleeds - but I have no power to solace! - o ye, who revel in affluance, see the afflictions of humanity and bestow your superfluity to ease them. Say not, we have suffered also, and thence withhold your compassion. What are your sufferings compared to those? - ye have still more than enough left. Act wisely - succour the miserable and lay up a treasure in Heaven.

I am afraid, Sir, you will think this description more the effort of imagination than a true picture of realities. But I can affirm with the greatest truth, that there is not a single circumstance touched upon, which I have not absolutely been an eye witness to.[88]

Subject and Comment: **Fruits of Revolution. Man Not Made for Rein and Spur.**

Hamilton: The world has its eye upon America. The noble struggle we have made in the cause of

[87] Written by Hamilton in his early teens. Appeared in the Royal Danish-American Gazette, October 3, 1772.
[88] Ibid

liberty has occasioned a kind of revolution in human sentiment. The influence of our example has penetrated the gloomy regions of despotism, and has pointed the way to inquiries which may shake it to its deepest foundations. Men begin to ask, every where: Who is this tyrant that dares to build his greatness on our misery and degradation? What commission has he to sacrifice millions to the wanton appetites of himself and a few minions that surround his throne?

To ripen enquiry into action, it remains for us to justify the revolution by its fruits.

If the consequences prove that we really have asserted the cause of human happiness, what may not be expected from so illustrious an example? In a greater or less degree the world will bless and imitate.

But if experience, in this instance, verifies the lesson long taught by the enemies of liberty, that the bulk of mankind are not fit to govern themselves; that they must have a master, and were only made for the rein and spur; we shall then see the final triumph of despotism over liberty; the advocates of the latter must acknowledge it to be an ignis fatuus, and abandon the pursuit. With the greatest advantages for promoting it that ever a people had, we shall have betrayed the cause of human nature.[89]

Subject and Comment: **Universal Civilization. Differences in Features and Complexions.**

Paine: It is not for us to enquire why, in the creation of mankind, the inhabitants of the several parts of the earth were distinguished by a difference in feature or complexion. It is sufficient to know that all are the work of the Almighty Hand. . . We esteem it a peculiar blessing granted to us, that we are enabled this day to add one more step to universal civilization, by removing, as much as possible, the sorrows of those, who have lived in undeserved bondage, and from which, by the assumed authority of the Kings of Great Britain, no longer

[89] Letter to citizens of New York, 1784.

effectual legal relief could be obtained. . . . We find our hearts enlarged with kindness and benevolence towards men of all conditions and nations; and we conceive ourselves at this particular period called upon by the blessings which we have received, to manifest the sincerity of our profession, and to give a substantial proof of our gratitude.[90]

Subject and Comment: **Reason and the Word of God**

Paine: . . . my endeavors have been directed to bring man to a right use of the reason that God has given him; to impress on him the great principles of divine morality, justice, and mercy, and a benevolent disposition to all men, and to all creatures; and to inspire in him a spirit of trust, confidence and consolation, in his Creator, unshackled by the fables of books pretending to be the word of God.[91]

Subject and Comment: **Word of God and Almighty Power**

Paine: What is it we want to know? Does not the creation, the universe we behold, preach to us the existence of an Almighty power, that governs and regulates the whole? And is not the evidence that this creation holds out to our senses infinitely stronger than any thing we can read in a book that any imposter might make and call the word of God? As for morality, the knowledge of it exists in every man's conscience.[92]

Subject and Comment: **Deism and Bibles**

Paine: Deism then teaches us, without the possibility of being deceived, all that is necessary or proper to be known. The creation is the Bible of the Deist. He there reads, in the hand-writing of the Creator himself, the certainty of his existence, and the immutability of his power; and all other Bibles

[90] From preamble to Pennsylvania's anti-slavery act.
[91] Cousins, supra, pp. 393-394.
[92] From The Age of Reason.

and Testaments are to him forgeries. The probability that we may be called to account hereafter, will, to reflecting minds, have the influence of belief; for it is not our belief or disbelief that can make or unmake the fact. As this is the state we are in, and which it is proper we should be in, as free agents, it is the fool only, and not the philosopher, nor even the prudent man, that will live as if there were no God. . . .[93]

Subject and Comment: **Revelation and Detestable Wickedness**

Paine: Though, speaking for myself, I admit the possibility of revelation, I totally disbelieve that the Almighty ever did communicate any thing to man, by any mode of speech, in any language, or by any kind of vision, or appearance, or by any means which our senses are capable of receiving, otherwise than by the universal display of himself in the works of the creation, and by that repugnance we feel in ourselves to bad actions, and disposition to good ones.

The most detestable wickedness, the most horrid cruelties, and the greatest miseries, that have afflicted the human race, have had their origin in this thing called revelation, or revealed religion. It has been the most dishonorable belief against the character of the divinity, the most destructive to morality, and the peace and happiness of man, that ever was propagated since man began to exist.[94]

Subject and Comment: **Bible Stories**

Paine: If these stories are false we err in believing them to be true, and ought not to believe them. It is therefore a duty which every man owes to himself, and reverentially to his Maker, to ascertain by every possible inquiry whether there be a sufficient evidence to believe them or not.

My own opinion is, decidedly, that the evidence does not warrant the belief, and that we sin in

[93] From **The Age of Reason.**
[94] Ibid.

forcing that belief upon ourselves and upon others. In saying this I have no other object in view than truth. But that I may not be accused of resting upon bare assertion, with respect to the equivocal state of the Bible, I will produce an example,[95] and I will not pick and cull the Bible for the purpose.

Subject and Comment: **Contradictory Character of Creator As Portrayed In Bible**

Paine: When we reflect on a sentence so tremendously severe as that of consigning the whole human race, eight person excepted, to deliberate drowning; a sentence, which represents the Creator in a more merciless character than any of those who we call Pagans ever represented the Creator to be, under the figure of any of their deities, we ought at least to suspend our belief of it, on a comparison of the beneficent character of the Creator with the tremendous severity of the sentence; but when we see the story told with such evident contradiction of circumstances, we ought to set it down for nothing better than a Jewish fable told by nobody knows whom and nobody knows when.

*   *   *

Had it come to us as an Arabic or Chinese book, and said to have been a sacred book by the people from whom it came, no apology would have been made for the confused and disorderly state it is in. The tales it relates of the Creator would have been censured, and our pity excited for those who believed them. We should have vindicated the goodness of God against such a book, and preached up the disbelief of it out of reverence to Him. . . .

*   *   *

It is therefore necessary that the book be examined; it is our duty to examine it; and to suppress the right of examination is sinful in any government, or in any judge or jury. The Bible makes God to

---

[95] Letter to Thomas Erskine, September of 1797.

say to Moses, Deut. vii. 2, "And when the Lord thy God shall deliver them before thee, thou shalt smite them, and utterly destroy them, thou shalt make no covenant with them, nor show mercy unto them."

Not all the priests, nor scribes, nor tribunals in the world, nor all the authority of man, shall make me believe that God ever gave such a Rose-perrian precept as that of showing no mercy; and consequently it is impossible that I or any person who believes as reverentially of the Creator as I do[96] can believe such a book to be the Word of God.

Subject and Comment: **Lasciviousness, Debauchery, and Infidelity**

Paine: Religion is a private affair between every man and his Maker, and no tribunal or third party has a right to interfere between them. It is not properly a thing of this world; it is only practiced in this world; but its object is in a future world; and it is not otherwise an object of just laws than for the purpose of protecting the equal rights of all, however various their belief may be.

If one man choose to believe the book called the Bible to be the Word of God, and another, from the convinced idea of the purity and perfection of God compared with the contradictions the book contains - from the lasciviousness of some of its stories, like that of Lot getting drunk and debauching his two daughters, which is not spoken of as a crime, and for which the most absurd apologies are made - from the immorality of some of its precepts, like that of showing no mercy- and from the total want of evidence on the case - thinks he ought not to believe it to be the Word of God, each of them has an equal right; and if the one has a right to give his reasons for believing it to be so, the other has an equal right to give his reasons for believing the contrary.

Anything that goes beyond this rule is an inquisition. Mr. Erskine talks of his moral education: Mr.

[96] Ibid.

Erskine is very little acquainted with theological subjects, if he does not know there is such a thing as a sincere and religious belief that the Bible is not the Word of God. This is my belief; it is the belief of thousands far more learned than Mr. Erskine; and it is a belief that is every day increasing. It is not infidelity, as Mr. Erskine profanely and abusively calls it; it is the direct reverse of infidelity. It is a pure religious belief, founded on the idea of the perfection of the Creator.[97]

Subject and Comment: **Universe As Bible**

Paine: Religion has two principal enemies, fanaticism and infidelity,, or that which is called atheism. The first requires to be combated by reason and morality, the other by natural philosophy.

The existence of a God is the first dogma of the Theophilanthropists. It is upon this subject that I solicit your attention; for though it has been often treated of, and that most sublimely, the subject is inexhaustible; and there will always remain something to be said that has not been before advanced. I go therefore to open the subject, and to crave your attention to the end.

The universe is the bible of the true Theophilanthropist. It is there that he reads of God. It is there that the proofs of His existence are to be sought and to be found. As to written or printed books, by whatever name they are called, they are the works of man's hands, and carry no evidence in themselves that God is the Author of any of them. It must be in something that man could not make that we must seek evidence for our belief, and that something is the universe, the true Bible - the inimitable work of God.

Contemplating the universe, the whole system of Creation, in this point of light, we shall discover, that all that which is called natural philosophy is properly a divine study. It is the study of God through His works. It is the best study, by which we can arrive at a knowledge of His existence, and the only one by which we can gain a glimpse

[97] Ibid.

of His perfection.

Do we want to contemplate His power? We see it in the immensity of the creation. Do we want to contemplate His wisdom? We see it in the unchangable order by which the incomprehensible WHOLE is governed. Do we want to contemplate His munificence? We see it in the abundance with which He fills the earth. Do we want to contemplate His mercy? We see it in His not withholding that abundance even from the unthankful. In fine, do we want to know what GOD is? Search not written or printed books, but the Scripture called the creation.

It has been the error of the schools to teach astronomy and all the other sciences and subjects of natural philosophy as accomplishments only; whereas they should be taught theologically, or with reference to the Being who is the Author of them: for all the principles of science are of divine origin. Man cannot make, or invent, or contrive principles; he can only discover them, and he ought to look through the discovery to the Author.

When we examine an extraordinary piece of machinery, an astonishing pile of architecture, a well executed statue, or a highly finished painting where life and action are imitated, and habit only prevents our mistaking a surface of light and shade for cubical solidity, or ideas are naturally led to think of the extensive genius and talents of the artist.

When we study the elements of geometry, we think of Euclid. When we speak of gravitation, we think of Newton. How then is it that when we study the works of God in the creation we stop short, and do not think of GOD? It is from the error of the schools in having taught those subjects as accomplishments only, and thereby separated the study of them from the Being who is the Author of them.

The schools have made the study of theology to consist in the study of opinions in written or printed books; whereas theology should be studied in the works or books of the Creation. The study of theology in books of opinions has often produced fanaticism, rancor and cruelty of temper; and from hence have proceeded the numerous persecutions, the fanatical quarrels, the religious burnings and massacres, that have desolated Europe.

But the study of theology in the works of the creation produces a direct contrary effect. The mind becomes at once enlightened and serene, a copy of the scene it beholds: information and adoration go hand in hand; and all the social faculties become enlarged.

The evil that has resulted from the error of the schools in teaching natural philosophy as an accomplishment only has been that of generating in the pupils a species of atheism. Instead of looking through the works of creation to the Creator himself, they stop short and employ the knowledge they acquire to create doubts of His existence. They labor with studied ingenuity to ascribe everything they behold to innate properties of matter, and jump over all the rest by saying that matter is eternal.

Let us examine this subject; it is worth examining; for if we examine it through all its cases, the result will be that the existence of a SUPERIOR CAUSE, or that which man calls GOD, will be discoverable by philosophical principles.

In the first place, admitting matter to have properties, as we see it has, the question still remains, how came matter by those properties? To this they will answer that matter possessed those properties eternally. This is not solution, but assertion; and to deny it is equally as impossible of proof as to assert it.

It is then necessary to go further; and therefore I say - if there exist a circumstance that is not a property of matter, and without which the universe, or to speak in a limited degree, the solar system composed of planets and a sun, could not exist a moment, all the arguments of atheism, drawn from properties of matter, and applied to account for the universe, will be overthrown, and the existence of a superior cause, or that which man calls God, becomes discoverable, as is before said, by natural philosophy.[98]

[98] The Existence of God, 1797.

Subject and Comment: **First Cause**

Paine: God is the power of first cause, nature is the law, and matter is the subject acted upon.[99]

Subject and Comment: **Prime Mover Preserves the System**

Paine: It sees upon the surface a perpetual decomposition and recomposition of matter. It sees that an oak produces an acorn, an acorn an oak, a bird an egg, an egg a bird, and so on. In things of this kind it sees something which it calls a natural cause, but none of the causes it sees is the cause of that motion which preserves the solar system.

Let us contemplate this wonderful and stupendous system consisting of matter, and existing by motion. It is not matter in a state of rest, nor in a state of decomposition or recomposition. It is matter systemized in perpetual orbicular or circular motion. As a system that motion is the life of it: as animation is life to an animal body, deprive the system of motion and, as a system, it must expire.

Who then breathed into the system the life of motion? What power impelled the planets to move, since motion is not a property of matter of which they are composed? If we contemplate the immense velocity of this motion, our wonder becomes increased, and our adoration enlarges itself in the same proportion.[100]

Subject and Comment: **When Power and Will Are Equal. Complicated Creeds.**

Paine: Where will infidelity, where will atheism, find cause for this astonishing velocity of motion, never ceasing, never varying, and which is the preservation of the earth in its orbit? It is not by reasoning from an acorn to an oak, from an egg to a bird, or from any change in the state of matter

[99] Ibid.

[100] Ibid.

on the surface of the earth, that this can be accounted for.

Its cause is not to be found in matter, nor in anything we call nature. The atheist who affects to reason, and the fanatic who rejects reason, plunge themselves alike into inextricable difficulties.

The one perverts the sublime and enlightening study of natural philosophy into a deformity of absurdities by not reasoning to the end. The other loses himself in the obscurity of metaphysical theories, and dishonors the Creator by treating the study of His works with contempt. The one is a half-rational of whom there is some hope, the other a visionary to whom we must be charitable.

When at first thought we think of a Creator, our ideas appear to us undefined and confused; but if we reason philosophically, those ideas can be easily arranged and simplified. It is a Being whose power is equal to His will.

Observe the nature of the will of man. It is of infinite quality. We cannot conceive the possibility of limits to the will. Observe, on the other hand, how exceedingly limited is his power of acting compared with the nature of his will. Suppose the power equal to the will, and man would be a God. He would will himself eternal, and be so. He could will a creation, and could make it.

In this progressive reasoning, we see in the nature of the will of man half of that which we conceive in thinking of God; add the other half, and we have the whole idea of a Being who could make the universe, and sustain it by perpetual motion; because He could create that motion.

We know nothing of the capacity of the will of animals, but we know a great deal of the difference of power, from a mite to a man.

Since then everything we see below us shows a progression of power, where is the difficulty in supposing that there is, at the summit of all things, a Being in whom an infinity of power unites with the infinity of the will? When this simple idea presents itself to our mind, we have the idea of a perfect Being that man calls God.

It is comfortable to live under the belief of the

existence of an infinite protecting power; and it
is an addition to that comfort to know that such
a belief is not a mere conceit of the imagination,
as many of the theories that are called religious
are; nor a belief founded only on tradition or received opinion; but is a belief deducible by the action
of reason upon the things that compose the system
of the universe; a belief arising out of visible facts.
So demonstrable is the truth of this belief that
if no such belief had existed, the persons who now
controvert it would have been the persons who
would have produced and propagated it; because
by beginning to reason they would have been led
to reason progressively to the end, and thereby
have discovered that matter and the properties
it has will not account for the system of the universe, and that there must necessarily be a superior
cause.

It was the excess to which imaginary systems
of religion had been carried, and the intolerance,
persecutions, burnings and massacres they occasioned, that first induced certain persons to propagate
infidelity; thinking, that upon the whole it was
better not to believe at all than to believe a multitude of things and complicated creeds that occasioned so much mischief in the world.

But those days are past, persecution has ceased,
and the antidote then set up against it has no longer
even the shadow of apology. We profess, and we
proclaim in peace, the pure, unmixed, comfortable
and rational belief of a God as manifested to us
in the universe. We do this without any apprehension
of that belief being made a cause of persecution
as other beliefs have been, or of suffering persecution ourselves. To God, and not to man, are all
men to account for their belief.

It has been well observed, at the first institution
of this Society, that the dogmas it professes to
believe are from the commencement of the world;
that they are not novelties, but are confessedly
the basis of all systems of religion, however numerous and contradictory they may be.

All men in the outset of the religion they profess
are Theophilanthropists. It is impossible to form

any system of religion without building upon those principles, and therefore they are not sectarian principles, unless we suppose a sect composed of all the world.

I have said in the course of this discourse that the study of natural philosophy is a divine study, because it is the study of the works of God in the creation. If we consider theology upon this ground, what an extensive field of improvement in things both divine and human opens itself before us!

All the principles of science are of divine origin. It was not man that invented the principles on which astronomy, and every branch of mathematics, are founded and studied. It was not man that gave properties to the circle and the triangle. Those principles are eternal and immutable.

We see in them the unchangeable nature of the Divinity. We see in them immortality, an immortality existing after the material figures that express those properties are dissolved in dust.[101]

_____

Subject and Comment: **Ghosts, Witches, and Angels**

Paine: Every new religion, like a new play, requires a new apparatus of dresses and machinery, to fit the new characters it creates. The story of Christ in the New Testament brings a new being upon the stage, which it calls the Holy Ghost; and the story of Abraham, the father of the Jews, in the Old Testament, gives existence to a new order of beings it calls angels. There was no Holy Ghost before the time of Christ, nor angels before the time of Abraham.

We hear nothing of these winged gentlemen, till more than two thousand years, according to the Bible chronology, from the time they say the heavens, the earth and all therein were made. After this, they hop about as thick as birds in a grove. The first we hear of pays his addresses to Hagar in the wilderness; then three of them visit Sarah; another wrestles a fall with Jacob; and these birds of passage having found their way to earth and

_____
[101] Ibid.

back, and continually coming and going. They eat and drink, and up again to heaven.

*   *   *

From angels in the Old Testament we get to prophets, to witches, to seers of visions, and dreamers of dreams; and sometimes we are told, as in 1 Samuel ix, 15, that God whispers in the ear. At other times we are not told, how the impulse was given, or whether sleeping or waking. In 2 Samuel xxiv, I, it is said, "And again the anger of the Lord was kindled against Israel, and he moved David against them to say, Go number Israel and Judah." And in 1 Chronicles xxi, 1, when the same story is again related, it is said, "And Satan stood up against Israel, and moved David to number Israel."

Whether this was done sleeping or waking, we are not told, but it seems that David, whom they call "a man after God's own heart," did not know by what spirit he was moved; and as to the men called inspired penmen, they agree so well about the matter that in one book they say it was God, and in the other that it was the devil. . . .

The God of eternity and of all that is real, is not the god of passing dreams and shadows of man's imagination. The God of truth is not the god of fable; the belief of a god begotten and a god crucified, is a god blasphemed. It is making a profane use of reason.

I shall conclude this Essay on Dream with the first two verses of Ecclesiasticus xxxiv, one of the books of the Aprocrypha. "The hopes of man void of understanding are vain and false; and dreams lift up fools. Whoso regardeth dreams is like him that catcheth a shadow and followeth after the wind."[102]

Subject and Comment: **Christians, Deists, Heretics, and Idolators. Revelation and 700 Wives.**

Paine: The word religion is a word of forced application when used with respect to the worship of God.

[102] Essay of 1802.

The root of the word is the Latin verb ligo, to tie or bind. From ligo, comes religo, to tie or bind over again, to make more fast - from religo, come the substantive religio, which, with the addition of n makes the English substantive religion.

The French use the word properly: when a woman enters a convent she is called a novitiate, that is, she is upon trial or probation. When she takes the oath, she is called a religieuse, that is, she is tied or bound by that oath to the performance of it. We use the word in the same kind of sense when we say we will religiously perform the promise that we make.

But the word, without referring to its etymology, has, in the manner it is used, no definite meaning, because it does not designate what religion a man is of. There is the religion of the Chinese, of the Tartars, of the Brahmins, of the Persians, of the Jews, of the Turks, etc.

The word Christianity is equally as vague as the word religion. No two sectaries can agree what it is. It is lo here and lo there. The two principal sectaries, Papists and Protestants, have often cut each other's throats about it.

The Papists call the Protestants heretics, and the Protestants call the Papists idolators. The minor sectaries have shown the same spirit of rancor, but as the civil law restrains them from blood, they content themselves with preaching damnation against each other.

The word protestant has a positive signification in the sense it is used. It means protesting against the authority of the Pope, and this is the only article in which the Protestants agree. In every other sense, with respect to religion, the word protestant is as vague as the word Christian.

When we say an Episcopalian, a Presbyterian, a Baptist, a Quaker, we know what those persons are, and what tenets they hold; but when we say a "Christian," we know he is not a Jew nor a Mahometan, but we know not if he be a trinitarian or an anti-trinitarian, a believer in what is called the immaculate conception, or a disbeliever, a man of seven sacraments, or of two sacraments, or of none. The word "Christian" describes what a man is not, but not what he is.

The word theology, from Theos, the Greek word for God, and meaning the study and knowledge of God, is a word that strictly speaking belongs to Theists or Deists, and not to the Christians. The head of the Christian Church is the person called Christ, but the head of the Church of the Theists, or Deists, as they are more commonly called (from Deus, the Latin word for God), is God Himself; and therefore the word "Theology" belongs to that Church which has Theos or God for its head, and not to the Christian Church which has the person called Christ for its head. Their technical world is Christianity, and they cannot agree on what Christianity is.

The words revealed religion and natural religion also require explanation. They are both invented terms, contrived by the Church for the support of its priestcraft. With respect to the first, there is no evidence of any such thing, except in the universal revelation that God has made of His power, His wisdom, His goodness, in the structure of the universe, and in all the works of creation.

We have no cause for ground from anything we behold in those works to suppose that God would deal partially by mankind, and reveal knowldedge to one nation and withhold it from another, and then damn them for not knowing it. The sun shines an equal quantity of light all over the world - and mankind in all ages and countries are endued with reason, and blessed with sight, to read the visible works of God in the creation, and so intelligent is the book that he that runs may read.

We admire the wisdom of the ancients, yet they had no Bibles nor books called "revelation." They cultivated the reason that God gave them, studied Him in His works, and arose to eminence.

As to the Bible, whether true or fabulous, it is a history, and history is not a revelation. If Solomon had seven hundred wives, and three hundred concubines, and if Sampson slept in Delilah's lap, and she cut his hair off, the relation of those things is mere history that needed no revelation from heaven to tell it; neither does it need any revelation to tell us that Samson was a fool for his pains, and Solomon too.

As to the expressions so often used in the Bible, that the word of the Lord came to such an one, or such an one, it was the fashion of speaking in those times, like the expression used by a Quaker, that the spirit moveth him, or that used by priests, that they have a call. We ought not to be deceived by phrases because they are ancient. But if we admit the supposition that God would condescend to reveal Himself in words, we ought not to believe it would be in such idle and profligate stories as are in the Bible; and it is for this reason, among others which our reverence to God inspires, that the Deists deny that the book called the Bible is the Word of God, or that it is revealed religion.

With respect to the term natural religion, it is upon the face of it, the opposite of artificial religion, and it is impossible for any man to be certain that what is called revealed religion is not artificial.

Man has the power of making books, inventing stories of God, and calling them revelation, or the Word of God. The Koran exists as an instance that this can be done, and we must be credulous indeed to suppose that this is the only instance and Mahomet the only imposter. The Jews could match him, and the Church of Rome could overmatch the Jews. The Mahometans believe the Koran, the Christians believe the Bible, and it is education [that] makes all the difference.

Books, whether Bibles or Korans, carry no evidence of being the work of any other power than man. It is only that which man cannot do that carries the evidence of being the work of a superior power. Man could not invent and make a universe - he could not invent nature, for nature is of divine origin. It is the laws by which the universe is governed.

When, therefore, we look through nature up to nature's God, we are in the right road of happiness, but when we trust to books as the Word of God, and confide in them as revealed religion, we are afloat on the ocean of uncertainty, and shatter into contending factions. The term, therefore, natural religion, explains itself to be divine religion, and the term revealed religion involves in it the suspicion of being artificial.

To show the necessity of understanding the meaning of words, I will mention an instance of a minister, I believe of the Episcopalian Church of Newark, in [New] Jersey. He wrote and published a book, and entitled it "An Antidote to Deism." An antidote to Deism must be Atheism. It has no other anti-dote - for what can be an antidote to the belief of a God, but the disbelief of God? Under the tuition of such pastors, what but ignorance and false information can be expected?[103]

Subject and Comment: **Various Books. Everyone A Deist. Divine Gift of Reason.**

Paine: Every person, of whatever religious denomination he may be, is a Deist in the first article of his Creed. Deism, from the Latin word Deus, God, is the belief of a God, and this belief is the first article of every man's creed.

It is on this article, universally consented to by all mankind, that the Deist builds his church, and here he rests. Whenever we step aside from this article, by mixing it with articles of human invention, we wander into a labyrinth of uncertainty and fable, and become exposed to every kind of imposition by pretenders to revelation.

The Persian shows the Zend-Avesta of Zoroaster, the lawgiver of Persia, and calls it the divine law; the Brahmin shows the Shaster, revealed, he says, by God to Brahma, and given to him out of a cloud; the Jew shows what he calls the Law of Moses, given, he says, by God, on the Mount Sinai; the Christian shows a collection of books and epistles, written by nobody knows who, and called the New Testament; and the Mahometan shows the Koran, given, he says, by God to Mahomet: each of these calls itself revealed religion, and the only true Word of God, and this the followers of each profess to believe from the habit of education, and each

[103] From **The Prospect** of 1804.

believes the others are imposed upon.

But when the divine gift of reason begins to expand itself in the mind and calls man to reflection, he then reads and contemplates God and His works, and not the books pretending to be revelation. The creation is the Bible of the true believer in God. Everything in this vast volume inspires him with sublime ideas of the Creator. The little and paltry, and often obscene, tales of the Bible sink into wretchedness when put in comparison with this mighty work.

The Deist needs none of those tricks and shows called miracles to confirm his faith, for what can be a greater miracle than the creation itself and his own existence?

There is happiness in Deism, when rightly understood, that is not to be found in any other system of religion. All other systems have something in them that either shock our reason, or are repugnant to it, and man, if he thinks at all, must stifle his reason in order to force himself to believe them.

But in Deism our reason and our belief become happily united. The wonderful structure of the universe, and everything we behold in the system of creation, prove to us, far better than books can do, the existence of a God, and at the same time proclaim His attributes.

It is by the exercise of our reason that we are enabled to contemplate God in His works, and imitate Him in His way. When we see His care and goodness extended over all His creatures, it teaches us our duty toward each other, while it calls forth our gratitude to Him. It is by forgetting God in His works, and running after the books of pretended revelation, that man has wandered from the straight path of duty and happiness, and become by turns the victim of doubt and the dupe of delusion.[104]

Subject and Comment: **Communion, Falsehoods and Resurrections from the Dead**

Paine: I have read in the newspapers your account of the visit you made to the unfortunate General

[104] Cousins, supra, pp. 430-431.

Hamilton, and of administering to him a ceremony of your church which you call the Holy Communion.

I regret the fate of General Hamilton, and I so far hope with you that it will be a warning to thoughtless man not to sport away the life that God has given him; but with respect to other parts of your letter I think it very reprehensible, and betrays great ignorance of what true religion is. But you are a priest, you get your living by it, and it is not your worldly interest to undeceive yourself.

After giving an account of your administering to the deceased what you call the Holy Communion, you add, "By reflecting on this melancholy event let the humble believer be encouraged ever to hold fast that precious faith which is the only source of true consolation in the last extremity of nature. Let the infidel be persuaded to abandon his opposition to the Gospel."

To show you, Sir, that your promise of consolation from Scripture has no foundation to stand upon, I will cite to you one of the greatest falsehoods upon record, and which was given, as the record says, for the purpose, and as a promise, of consolation.

In the epistle called the First Epistle of Paul to the Thessalonians, iv, the writer consoles the Thessalonians as to the case of their friends who were already dead.

He does this by informing them, and he does it he says, by the word of the Lord (a most notorious falsehood), that the general resurrection of the dead and the ascension of the living will be in his and their days; that their friends will then come to life again; that the dead in Christ will rise first. - "Then we (says he, ver. 17, 18) which are alive and remain shall be caught up together with THEM in the clouds, to meet the Lord in the air, and so shall we ever be with the Lord. Wherefore comfort one another with these words."

Delusion and falsehood cannot be carried higher than they are in this passage. You, Sir, are but a novice in the art. The words admit of no equivocation. The whole passage is in the first person and the present tense, "We which are alive."

Had the writer meant a future time, and a distant generation, it must have been in the third person and the future tense. "They who shall then be alive." I am thus particular for the purpose of nailing you down to the text, that you may not ramble from it, nor put other constructions upon the words than they will bear, which priests are very apt to do.

Now, Sir, it is impossible for serious man, to whom God has given the divine gift of reason, and who employs that reason to reverence and adore the God that gave it, it is, I say, impossible for such a man to put confidence in a book that abounds with fable and falsehood as the New Testament does. This passage is but a sample of what I could give you.

You call on those whom you style "infidels" (and they in return might call you an idolator, a worshiper of false gods, a preacher of false doctrines), "to abandon their opposition to the Gospel." Prove, Sir, the Gospel to be true, and the opposition will cease of itself; but until you do this (which we know you cannot do) you have no right to expect they will notice your call. If by infidels you mean Deists (and you must be exceedingly ignorant of the origin of the word Deist, and know but little of Deus, to put that construction upon it), you will find yourself overmatched if you begin to engage in a controversy with them.

Priests may dispute with priests, and sectaries with sectaries, about the meaning of what they agree to call Scripture, and end as they began; but when you engage with a Deist you must keep to fact. Now, Sir, you cannot prove a single article of your religion to be true, and we tell you so publicly. Do it if you can. The Deistical article, the belief of a God, with which your creed begins, has been borrowed by your church from the ancient Deists, and even this article you dishonor by putting a dream-begotten phantom which you call His son, over His head, and treating God as if he was super-annuated.

Deism is the only profession of religion that admits of worshiping and reverencing God in purity, and the only one on which the thoughtful mind can repose with undisturbed tranquility. God is almost forgotten in the Christian religion. Everything, even the creation, is ascribed to the son of Mary.

In religion, as in everything else, perfection consists in simplicity. The Christian religion of Gods with Gods, like wheels within wheels, is like a complicated machine that never goes right, and every projector in the art of Christianity is trying to mend it. It is its defects that have caused such a number and variety of tinkers to be hammering at it, and still it goes wrong.

In the visible world no time-keeper can go equally true with the sun; and in like manner, no complicated religion can be equally true with the pure and unmixed religion of Deism.

Had you not offensively glanced at a description of men whom you call by a false name, you would not have been troubled nor honored with this address; neither has the writer of it any desire or intention to enter into controversy with you. He thinks the temporal establishment of your church politically unjust and offensively unfair; but with respect to religion itself; distinct from temporal establishments; he is happy in the enjoyment of his own, and he leaves you to make the best you can of yours.[105]

Subject and Comment: **Jeffersonian Christianity**

Jefferson: I am a Christian in the only sense in which I believe Jesus wished anyone to be, sincerely attached to his doctrine in preference to all others; ascribing to him all human excellence, and believing that he never claimed any other.[106]

Subject and Comment: **Miracles True and False**

Paine: In the same sense that every thing may be said to be a mystery, so also may it be said that every thing is a miracle, and that no one thing is greater than another. The elephant, though larger, is not a greater miracle than a mite; nor a mountain

---

105 Letter to Bishop Moore. See: Cousins, supra, p. 436.
106 Letter to Benjamin Rush. Ibid, 117.

a greater miracle than an atom. To an almighty power it is no more difficult to make the one than the other, and no more difficult to make a million of worlds than to make one. Every thing, therefore, is a miracle, in one sense; whilst, in the other sense, there is no such thing as a miracle. It is a miracle when compared to our power, and our comprehension. It is not a miracle compared to the power that performs it. But as nothing in this description conveys the idea that is affixed to the word miracle, it is necessary to carry the inquiry further.

Mankind have conceived to themselves certain laws, by which what they call nature is supposed to act; and that a miracle is something contrary to the operation and effect of those laws. But unless we know the whole extent of those laws, and of what are commonly called the powers of nature, we are not able to judge whether any thing that may appear to us as wonderful or miraculous, be within, or beyond, or contrary to, her natural power of acting.

The ascension of a man several miles high into the air, would have everything in it that constitutes the idea of a miracle, if it were not known that a species of air can be generated several times lighter than the common atmospheric air, and yet possess elasticity enough to prevent the balloon, in which that light air is enclosed, from being compressed into as many times less bulk, by the common air that surrounds it. In like manner, extracting flashes or sparks of fire from the human body, as visibly as from a steel struck with a flint, and causing iron or steel to move without any visible agent, would also give the idea of a miracle, if we were not acquainted with electricity and magnetism; so also would many other experiments in natural philosophy, to those who are not acquainted with the subject. The restoring persons to life who are to appearance dead, as is practiced upon drowned persons, would also be a miracle, if it were not known that animation is capable of being suspended without being extinct.[107]

[107] From **The Age of Reason.**

Subject and Comment: **What Good is Grief?**

Jefferson: My hopes, indeed, sometimes fail; but not oftener than the forebodings of the gloomy. There are, I acknowledge, even in the happiest life, some terrible convulsions, heavy set-offs against the opposite page of the account. I have often wondered for what good end the sensations of grief could be intended. All our other passions, within proper bounds have an useful opposite. And the perfection of the moral character is, not in stoical apathy, so hypocritically vaunted, and so untruly too, because impossible, but in a just equilibrium of all the passions. I wish the pathologists then would tell us what is the use of grief in the economy, and of what good it is in the cause, proximate or remote.[108]

Subject and Comment: **Openly Defend Your Position**

Adams: Heard Mr. Mccarty all day. Spent the evening and supped at Mr. Green's with Thayer. Honesty, sincerity, and openness I esteem essential marks of a good mind. I am, therefore, of opinion that men ought (after they have examined with unbiased judgments every system of religion, and chosen one system, on their own authority, for themselves), to avow their opinions and defend them with boldness.[109]

Subject and Comment: **Cartloads of Trumpery**

Adams: Spent an hour in the beginning of the evening at Major Gardiner's where it was thought that the design of Christianity was not to make men good riddle-solvers, or good mystery-mongers, but good men, good magistrates, and good subjects, good husbands and good wives, good parents and good children, good masters and good servants. The follow-

---

[108] Letter to John Adams, April 8, 1816.
[109] Adam's diary, March 7, 1756.

ing questions may be answered some time or other, namely - Where do we find a precept in the Gospel requiring Ecclesiastical Synods? Convocations? Councils? Decrees? Creeds? Confessions? Oaths? Subscriptions? and whole cartloads of other trumpery that we find religion encumbered with in these days?[110]

Subject and Comment: **Millions of Fables**

Adams: . . . millions of fables, tales, legends have been blended with both Jewish and Christian revelation that have made them the most bloody religion that ever existed.[111]

Subject and Comment: **Return of Jesus**

Adams: I thank you for your favor of the 12th instant. Hope springs eternal. Eight millions of Jews hope for a Messiah more powerful and glorious than Moses, David, or Solomon; who is to make them as powerful as he pleases. Some hundreds of millions of Musslemen expect another prophet more powerful than Mahomet, who is to spread Islamism over the whole earth. Hundreds of millions of Christians expect and hope for a millennium in which Jesus is to reign for a thousand years over the whole world before it is burnt up. The Hindoos expect another and final incarnation of Vishnu, who is to do great and wonderful things, I know not what. All these hopes are founded on real or pretended revelation. The modern Greeks, too, it seems, hope for a deliverer who is to produce them - the Themistocleses and Demostheneses - Platos and Aristotles - the Solons and Lycurguses. On what prophecies they found their belief, I know not. You and I hope for splendid improvements in human society, and vast amelioration in the condition of mankind. Our faith may be supposed by more rational arguments than any of the former,

[110] Adam's diary, February 18, 1756.
[111] Ccusins, supra, P. 75.

I own that I am very sanguine in the belief of them, as I hope you are, and your reasoning in your letter confirmed me in them.[112]

Subject and Comment: **Of Priests and Infidels**

Jefferson: By the same test the world must judge me. But this does not satisfy the priesthood. They must have a positive, a declared assent to all their interested absurdities. My opinion is that there would never have been an infidel, if there had never been a priest. The artificial structures they have built on the purest of all moral systems, for the purpose of deriving from it pence and power, revolts those who think for themselves, and who read in that system only what is really there. These, therefore, they brand with such nick-names as their enmity chooses gratuitously to impute.[113]

Subject and Comment: **Loathsome Combination of Church and State**

Jefferson: I abuse the priests, indeed, who have so much abused the pure and holy doctrines of their master, and who have laid me under no obligations of reticence as to the tricks of their trade. The genuine system of Jesus, and the artificial structures they have erected, to make them the instruments of wealth, power, and preeminence to themselves, are as distinct things in my view as light and darkness; and while I have classed them with soothsayers and necromancers, I place him among the greatest reformers of morals, and scourges of priestcraft that have ever existed. They felt him as such, and never rested until they had silenced him by death. But his heresies against Judaism prevailing in the long run, the priests have tacked about, and rebuilt upon them the temple which he destroyed, as splendid, as profitable, and as imposing as that.

Government, as well as religion, has furnished

[112] Letter to Thomas Jefferson, September 24, 1821.
[113] Letter to Mrs. Harrison Smith, August 6, 1816.

its schisms, its persecutions, and its devices for flattering idleness on the earnings of the people. It has its hierarchy of emperors, kings, princes, and nobles, as that has of popes, cardinals, archbishops, bishops, and priests. In short, cannibals are not to be found in the wilds of America only, but are revelling on the blood of every living people. Turning, then, from this loathsome combination of Church and State, and weeping over the follies of our fellow men, who yield themselves the willing dupes and drudges of these mountebanks, I consider reformation and redress as desperate, and abandon them to the Quixotism of more enthusiastic minds.[114]

Subject and Comment: **Quakers Without Priests**

Jefferson: We should all then, like the Quakers, live without an order of priests, moralize for ourselves, follow the oracle of conscience, and say nothing about what no man can understand, nor therefore believe; for I suppose belief to be the assent of the mind to an intelligible proposition.[115]

Subject and Comment: **Plato and Christianity**

Jefferson: The Christian priesthood, finding the doctrines of Christ levelled to every understanding, and too plain to need explanation, saw in the mysticism of Plato materials with which they might build up an artificial system, which might, from its indistinctness, admit everlasting controversy, give employment for their order, and introduce it to profit, power and pre-eminence. The doctrines which flowed from the lips of Jesus himself are within the comprehension of a child; but thousands of volumes have not yet explained the Platonisms engrafted on them; and for this obvious reason, that nonsense can never be explained.[116]

Subject and Comment: **God of Nature or Fictitious Miracles**

[114] Letter to Charles Clay, January 29, 1815.
[115] Letter to John Adams, August 22, 1813.
[116] Letter to John Adams, July 5, 1814.

Adams: The question before the human race is, whether the God of Nature shall govern the world by his own laws, or whether priests and kings shall rule it by fictitious miracles? Or, in other words, whether authority is originally in the people? or whether it has descended for 1800 years in a succession of popes and bishops, or brought down from heaven by the Holy Ghost in the form of a dove, in a phial of holy oil?[117]

Subject and Comment: **Rack, Wheel, Fire, and Hot Poker**

Adams: We think ourselves possessed, or, at least, we boast that we are so, of liberty of conscience on all subjects, and of the right of free inquiry and private judgment in all cases, and yet how far are we from these exalted privileges in fact. There exists, I believe, throughout the whole Christian world, a law which makes it blasphemy to deny, or to doubt the divine inspiration of all the books of the Old and New Testaments, from Genesis to Revelations. In most countries of Europe it is punished by fire at the stake, or the rack, or the wheel. In England itself, it is punished by boring through the tongue with a red-hot poker.

In America it is not much better; even in our own Massachusetts, which I believe, upon the whole, is as temperate and moderate in religious zeal as most of the States, a law was made in the latter end of the last century, repealing the cruel punishments of the former laws, but substituting fine and imprisonment upon all those blasphemers upon any book of the Old Testament or New.

Now, what free inquiry, when a writer must surely encounter the risk of fine or imprisonment for adducing any argument for investigation into the divine authority of those books? Who would run the risk of translating Dupuis? I cannot enlarge upon the subject, though I have it much at heart. I think such laws a great embarrassment, great obstructions to the improvement of the human mind. Books that cannot bear examination, certainly ought

[117] Letter to Thomas Jefferson, June 20, 1815.

not to be established as divine inspiration by penal laws.

It is true, few persons appear desirous to put such laws in execution, and it is also true that some few persons are hardy enough to venture to depart from them. But as long as they continue in force as laws, the human mind must make an awkward and clumsy progress in its investigations. I wish they were repealed. The substance and essence of Christianity, as I understand it, is eternal and unchangeable, and will bear examination forever, but it has been mixed with extraneous ingredients, which I think will not bear examination, they ought to be separated.[118]

Subject and Comment: **Benjamin Franklin Not Saved?**

Franklin: Some of Mr. Whitefield's enemies affected to suppose that he would apply these collections to his own private emolument; but I, who was intimately acquainted with him (being employed in printing his Sermons and Journals, etc.), never had the least suspicion of his integrity, but am to this day decidedly of opinion that he was in all his conduct a perfectly honest man; methinks my testimony in his favor ought to have the more weight, as we had no religious connection. He used, indeed, sometimes to pray for my conversion, but never had the satisfaction of believing that his prayers were heard. Ours was a mere civil friendship, sincere on both sides, and lasted to his death.[119]

Subject and Comment: **Not All Governments Ordained of God**

Adams: Massachusetts is then seized with a violent fit of anger at the clergy. It is curious to observe the conduct of the tories towards this sacred body. If a clergyman, of whatever character, preaches against the principles of the revolution, and tells the people that, upon pain of damnation, they must submit to an established government, the tories

[118] Letter to Thomas Jefferson, January 23, 1825.
[119] From Franklin's autobiography. See: Cousins, supra, p. 38.

cry him up as an excellent man and a wonderful preacher, invite him to their tables, procure him missions from the society and chaplainships to the navy, and flatter him with the hopes of lawn sleeves.

But if a clergyman preaches Christianity, and tells the magistrates that they were not distinguished from their brethren for their private emolument, but for the good of the people; that the people are bound in conscience to obey a good government, but are not bound to submit to one that aims at destroying all the ends of government,-oh sedition! treason!

The clergy in all ages and countries, and in this in particular, are disposed enough to be on the side of government as long as it is tolerable. If they have not been generally in the late administration on that side, it is a demonstration that the late administration has been universally odious. The clergy of this province are a virtuous, sensible, and learned set of men, and they do not take their sermons from newspapers, but the Bible; unless it be a few, who preach passive obedience. These are not generally curious enough to read Hobbes. It is the duty of the clergy to accommodate their discourses to the times, to preach against such sins as are most prevalent, and recommend such virtues as are most wanted. For example,-if exorbitant ambition and venality are predominant, ought they not to warn their hearers against those vices? If public spirit is much wanted, should they not inculcate this great virtue? If the rights and duties of Christian magistrates and subjects are disputed, should they not explain them, show their nature, ends , limitations, and restrictions, how much soever it may move the gall of Massachusettensis?[120]

Subject and Comment: **Bigotry A Disease of Ignorance**

Jefferson: Bigotry is the disease of ignorance, of morbid minds; enthusiasm of the free and buoyant. Education and free discussion are the antidotes of both.[121]

[120] Letter to **Boston Gazette** in 1774.
[121] Letter to John Adams, August 1, 1816.

Subject and Comment: **The Great and Universal Element**

Adams: Will you be so good as to give me a logical, mathematical, or moral, or any other definition of this phrase, "moral liberty;" and to tell me who is to exercise this "liberty;" and by what principle or system of morality it is to be exercised? Is not this liberty and morality to reside in the great and universal element, "THE PEOPLE?" Have they not always resided there? And will they not always reside there?

This moral liberty resides in Hindoos and Mahometans, as well as in Christians; in Cappadocian monarchists, as well as in Athenian democrats; in Shaking Quakers, as well as in the General Assembly of the Presbyterian clergy; in Tartars and Arabs, Negroes and Indians, as well as in the people of the United States of America.[122]

Subject and Comment: **Bigotry, Fanaticism, and Those Ultra Christian Sects**

Jefferson: But the greatest of all reformers of the depraved religion of his own country, was Jesus of Nazareth. Abstracting what is really his from the rubbish in which it is buried, easily distinguished by its lustre from the dross of his biographers, and as separable from that as the diamond from the dunghill, we have the outlines of a system of the most sublime morality which has ever fallen from the lips of man; outlines which it is lamentable he did not live to fill up. Epictetus and Epicurus give laws for governing ourselves, Jesus a supplement of the duties and charities we owe others. The establishment of the innocent and genuine character of this benevolent moralist, and the rescuing it from the imputation of imposture, which has resulted from artificial systems, invented by ultra-Christian sects, unauthorized by a single word ever uttered by him, is a most desirable object, and one to

[122] Letter to John Taylor, (no. 13) 1814.

which Priestley has successfully devoted his labors
and learning. It would in time, it is to be hoped,
effect a quiet euthanasia of the heresies of bigotry
and fanaticism which have so long triumphed over
human reason, and so generally and deeply afflicted
mankind; but this work is to be begun by winnowing
the grain from the chaff of the historians of his
life. I have sometimes thought of translating
Epictetus (for he has never been tolerable translated
into English) by adding the genuine doctrines of
Epicurus from the Syntagma of Gassendi, and an
abstract from the Evangelists of whatever has
the stamp of the eloquence and fine imagination
of Jesus.[123]

Subject and Comment: **Sacred Rights of Mankind**

Hamilton: The Sacred Rights of Mankind are not
to be rummaged for among old parchments or musty
records. They are written, as with a sunbeam,
in the whole volume of human nature, by the Hand
of the Divinity itself, and can never be erased
or obscured by moral power.[124]

[123] Letter to William Short, October 31, 1819.
[124] Cousins, supra, p. 326.

... PRIESTLEY was successful... is with his later
... writings, it would appear that it is to the point
...ect... chief exponents of the changes of history
and tradition which have so long triumphed over
human reason, and so thoroughly and nearly different
his aim; but this work is to carry on by weakening
the... notions the minds of the superstition of his
... will have something, through or publishing...
Epicurus that he has never been reliable than the
into... induced by adding new, vigorous doctrines, of
Epicurus from the systems of Crassus, and in
restitution. The Frenchman's to gather the
the... of the devotions... and... the resolution
France.

Subject and Controlling Stated Forms of Mankind.

Duplicate: The barred, Rights of Mankind appears
to be common, be remove, for experimentation, but a
record. They have written, as with a control,
in the whole volume of human nature, by the fact
that the furnace itself, but otherwise has gained
or acquired by mind power.

THE

WAY

IT

IS

The Fundamentalist Threat

We have examined excerpts from the writings of seven of the key players in the birth-drama of this nation. Not included are Samuel Adams, John Dickinson, Philip Freneau, Patrick Henry, John Jay, Gouverneur Morris, James Otis, Benjamin Rush, Charles Pinckney, Roger Sherman, James Wilson, and others, who were also leaders. Yet an examination of their views would not substantially alter the picture of ideas presented by those covered.

The men we considered do comprise a highly select group in the sense that included is the author of the Declaration of Independence; the first Secretary of the Treasury; the presiding officer at the Constitutional Convention; the "Father of His Country"; the "Father of the Constitution"; our most illustrious diplomat, and the man whose writings are said to have begun the concerted movement in this country toward independence. Among this select group are the first four Presidents of the United States. By any reasonable standard we have included those who played the most vital roles in shaping the attitudes of all involved in the birth of our nation.

These were reasoning, intelligent men who founded a country wherein ideas were to be freely held and expressed, particularly those regarding personal beliefs. Religion was to be free from state support; the people free from religious inquisitions and laws prescribing their peaceful religious conduct.

Revolutionaries

In our current anti-revolutionary fervor we forget our nation's Founding Fathers were revolutionaries. They rejected the fundamentalist religious concept that mankind is totally depraved. They trusted the good sense of the common man and, using this as a base, built a nation that was and is the envy of the world: So much so that others still seek a similar freedom from oppression.

Each march to freedom takes a different route. All seek deliverance from what Hamilton called "rein and spur." Unhappily we have become obsessed with the idea that shackles can only be removed through capitalism. Much of our own progress has come from government involvement in the economics of individual existence. Yet we hold pure capitalism up as a dogma that must be followed by those seeking freedom abroad; while, here at home, we have long since drifted - and to our advantage, in the main - from the laissez faire economics of Adam Smith. This emphasis on economics, rather than freedom, has brought our country to an all time high in disrespect among freedom lovers throughout the world. In their eyes, we stand for luxurious living. This is the reason so many foreigners want to come here; while, at the same time, we are so hated abroad. This strange paradox should be understood. It is clearly understandable. The day will surely come when our policy of basing support for freedom on such ephemeral foundations as race or economics will come home to haunt us. As we turn a deaf ear to the cries for freedom from non-capitalist movements abroad, we should not also be deaf to the political roar of the radical right within the United States.

In a misguided attempt to correct problems of national discontent, drug abuse, family dissolution- ment, and a general disquiet caused by unwise foreign adventurism, many have turned to the radical religious right in an attempt to regain lost and treasured values. While religion may be of great benefit, the radical right is steeped in bigotry. It threatens our educational system, and the freedoms that made this country great.

So long as these radicals rolled in the aisles and stayed in their churches, confining themselves to good works, they presented no pressing danger. Now they have become a national political force, and what many of them stand for should be generally known. The incidious threat they present is the subject of the discussions that follow.

Because of their seductive, highly emotional, show-biz attractiveness, some people have lost a sense for the proper use of reason and are going off the deep end in an ecclesiastical binge. This dive into religious fanaticism is clearly within the rights of those who wish to take the plunge. It is also within the rights of those opposed to their ideas not to vote for their candidates for public office. As a political machine the fanatical right, awash as it is in bigotry and ignorance, threatens our educational system, and the individual freedoms that made this country great.

As the people of the earth hunger for peace and food, religious fanaticism daily manifests itself throughout the world diverting minds and money from human needs. It is beginning to happen here, as abortion clinics are bombed, and in numerous other, less violent ways, our freedoms are under attack.

The very extremist views that brought our forebears to these shores are being resurrected in the name of patriotism and family values. The danger is that in this zeal to return to honorable standards of the past, we lose sight of the values we once placed on freedom and our ability to reason for ourselves.

Habits of critical thinking that caused men to question the divine right of kings, also caused our nation's Founding Fathers to question the doctrines of the church. They dared to bring reason into play where faith had stood alone. Reason was not seen as anti-religious, but as supportive of faith, albeit that faith was sometimes unorthodox.

Typically, the fanatic fundamentalist will see faith in an either-or frame; it is either good or bad. It's us and them. To him, good faith is like his own. There is no academic disagreement, but deep seated hostility for those who philosophically differ with him. The abortionist, pornographer, advocate of world government, supporter of the United Nations and women's rights, those who advocate peace and oppose capital punishment, are all considered subversive, Communist, agents of the Antichrist and - worst of all - "liberals."

How soon we forget that our key Founding Fathers were revolutionaries and religious liberals. Yet none was without faith. All believed in God. but none covered here - as stated earlier - would qualify as a "full gospel, evangelical charismatic" fundamentalist. They agreed that all humans are endowed by their creator with certain natural rights.

122 /

With the possible exception of Thomas Paine,[125] they felt government should keep clear of religious beliefs. Believer and non-believer were to be equal citizens, free from governmental interference in their personal religious views and the public expression of those views. While these Founding Fathers were religious liberals and revolutionaries, they are often presented by the right as orthodox Christian conservatives.

The Inquisition was fresh in their minds as were the excesses of Christians in this country after it began to be settled. The Founding Fathers were not averse to comment critically on religious institutions and practices from what they called "popery" to Quakerism. Criticism does not constitute bigotry. Quite the opposite. It is the bigot who opposes new ideas and critical thinking.

As our national debt soars into the trillions of dollars and we otherwise prostitute our resources in a futile attempt to secure our freedoms through armaments, we must not lose sight of the forces within seeking to change our system. They may be more fanatic and immediate than we realize, and they may be coming from a generally unsuspected source, the radical religious right.

The Brethren
While the Founding Fathers showed a common respect for the individual rights of all people, the religious fanatic is taught to "love the brethren and pray for the unsaved." If you argue from the Bible that it often seeks to direct its readers to have compassion and to love one's neighbors whomever they might be, you will get nowhere. To these fundamentalists, it's us and them, with "them" being the "unsaved," a term of opprobrium which applies to everyone - Catholics, Jews, even mainline Protestants - who don't agree with their dogma or otherwise meet their notions of one righteous before God.

If you are not "saved, and filled with the Holy Ghost with evidence of speaking in tongues," the Pentecostal charismatics will pray for you. You may be taken aback to learn that the prayer being

[125] Supra, p. 92. Compare with comments of Jefferson, pp. 13-15, supra.

lifted up in your behalf is that you will be physically or fiscally stricken to such an extent that you will be driven to your knees, repent of your sins, and be "saved."

Salvation in their frame of reference, sufficient to qualify a person as one to the "brethren," involves a certain ritual which generally follows this format: The guilt-ridden parishioner kneels at the altar accompanied by one or more certified believers. As they pray together, the one seeking to become one of the "brethren" is cajoled to "let it all out," or words to that effect. (Translation: Begin to babble.) There may be prolonged moments of attempts to "get it all out." When babbling begins, the preacher is called over to listen and in effect to certify that the sounds being made are "genuine." You know the suppliant has been duly approved as one of the "brethren" when the preacher gives a bone dry chuckle and, smiling paternalistically, lays his hands on the supplicant. At this point the new brother or sister may keel over in a swoon, being careful to fall into the arms of an official "catcher" who then lowers the supplicant - now "slain in the Spirit" - to the floor. On rising, the newly "saved" one is asked to testify. Usually a few words of joy are tearfully given that guilt has been lifted. (Building guilt and then providing its relief through "salvation" drives the church, and fills its collection plates.)

Feeling relieved of guilt, for a week or more thereafter, he or she may attend church, testify, and even come in off hours to do chores around the church building. By this time the preacher is but a little lower than the Deity - or at the very least, has super-saint status - in the eyes of the initiate, and the "salvation" process is now completed in the eyes of the congregation.

It is important to remember that even if one belongs to a mainline church, but has not followed this spirit filling, certifying process in a "full gospel, Bible believing, Pentecostal" church, his claim of salvation is suspect to most charismatic fundamentalists. Of course, this whole procedure, while emotionally lifting and exciting, bears closer resemblance to a fraternity or social club initiation than to a voluntary, reflective, heartfelt expression of belief arrived at over an extended period of time.

Most importantly, the seed is sown in the minds

of the congregation that those who have not followed such a routine are not good - at least not complete - Christians. They may grudgingly say that some mainliners are "saved," but you wonder if they mean it. According to their beliefs most people will eventually burn in hell because Jesus said - they remind you - that the gateway to heaven is narrow and few will enter. This is in sharp contrast to the high value placed on all people by the Founding Fathers, and by Jesus, if one reads the entire Sermon on the Mount[126] with an open mind.

In addition to the self-exalting ritual of certifying salvation, the "full gospel, evangelical, charismatic," fundamentalist preacher is called upon to do the more mundane tasks of dedicating children, performing marriages, visiting the sick, and officiating at funerals. It's all very heady stuff. Not well suited to genuine humility; well suited to feigned piety and exhalted self-esteem. So don't let those false smiles, hand holdings, and hugs fool you. Beneath that benign exterior may beat the heart of a mercenary, charlatan, and bigot.

Faith Healers

The manifest danger of the faith-healing, fundamentalist preacher is that he may use his exalted status to play upon the emotional dependency of his followers to their detriment. Delayed medical care can sometimes exacerbate an illness, even result in death. To the adoring parishioner, reliance on the healing hand of the Master, administered through one claiming to be a conduit for His powers, can be irresistible. What would you or I do if faced with a seemingly no-win medical situation? We would grasp at anything that held the slightest ray of hope for the alleviation of our pain and suffering. What, then, could be more logical than to turn in our distress to the all-time Winner. The "all-powerful One who cannot lose?" Certainly this is the mindset encouraged by these preachers. The opportunity for fraud is evident. The likelihood of relatives and loved ones being able to later prove fraud, remote to nonexistent.

Suppose the sick person seeking relief gives or

[126] Chapters 5, 6, and 7 of Matthew.

leaves all or a portion of his earthly wealth to the preacher or his church. The difficulty in having such a gift or bequest later set aside for fraud would be considerable. In the first place, there would be the natural reluctance of the decedents heirs to sue a church or "man of God." If such a suit were brought, the defendant could mount a multi-faceted defense. After all, people do die. Also the person administered to was probably certifiably seriously ill. It would be difficult to show he was not comforted in his last illness, possibly "saved." In the eyes of many jurors this would have more than compensated for the decedents gifts to his pastor and church, salvation being "more precious than gold." In addition, the preacher would likely have been circumspect in his relationship to the decedent. So there would probably be no tangible evidence of chicanery or fraud.

Deception and the Almighty's Dollar

Have you ever heard a religious broadcast in which the evangelist asked for a "contribution" of at least a minimal amount in order for his listeners to receive something? If not, you haven't been listening. A preacher might say he will send you his latest tape on "How to Overcome Materialism" if you send him a contribution of at least some given amount, say $50. Well that's no contribution, it's an offer to sell. Those who respond are making a purchase , not making a contribution, except for the amount in excess of the $50 purchase price. The entire amount is called a "contribution" by the preacher for tax purposes. Misrepresentations of this kind is daily fare on radio and TV gospel stations.

Ironically, Jesus probably told more parables inveighing against the possession of riches than against any other sin, with the possible exception of hypocrisy. For the preacher it then becomes necessary to soften and put a new twist on these words of the Lord; to tone them down so as not to offend rich people that might be or become financial supporters. So the dogma now in the churches is that Jesus really didn't preach against having wealth, it is the misuse of one's dollars that gets him in trouble upstairs. This goes over big. So many dream of wealth and are delighted to hear the preacher say their lusting is permissible. For those who have struck it rich, they may keep their money so long as they keep some of it going to the pastor and church. There is one small passage in the Bible, that amounts to no more than a greeting between friends, which is used in an attempt to show one and all that God really wants all Christians to have lots of money (3 John 2). Since it suits their purpose, this greeting has been used as a Deitific pronouncement of desire that all believers become materially prosperous.

It is reported that one TV evangelist bent on sustaining his political power was able to raise $1 million in one day. (Such reports are hard to verify as responsible audits and church business have not yet wed. They are not even courting.) Yet the time may come when we see one or more of these more successful money raisers listed among the Fortune 500. But no matter how much they get, they want more. They plead for money for all manner of causes. But the one that gets most attention is their need to meet the costs of TV and radio time. Reliance on divine Providence to supply their needs has long since been abandoned as ineffective. The beggars of the streets have been replaced by the beggars of the airwaves.

The Pentecostal holly roller is repeatedly told by his preacher that it is the sum total of all like-minded believers that constitutes the church of God. It is not the church building, they are told, but the body of believers that is the church. This doctrine holds until the money runs low. Then, miraculously, a transformation occurs. The church building becomes the church and the parishioners are told in no uncertain terms to bring their tithes into the storehouse.

Show-Biz Religion

No doubt this is the time when there has been a marriage of convenience between the entertainment business and the church. Never have the voices of so many leather-lunged orators and their entourages been projected so far and to so many potential contributors - all in living color. The devotees of shout and stomp religion can sit at home and catch the latest show. There is no pressing need now to hit the sawdust trail in search of religious entertainment. It's right there in the living room. Tents are fading. The clamor now is to get on TV, only then can one of these preachers feel he has arrived.

If the fundamentalist once eschewed the fleshly things of this earth, no more. For example, Paul's comments about the proper dress and conduct of women in church has long since been inundated in a flood of baubles and beads. For pure theatre, these shows are hard to beat. The thirst of the faithful for entertainment seems unquenchable.

The Role of Women

You can talk about your men of Gideon, you can talk about your men of Saul, but don't dare mention womens rights. No, sir! Women are not to be on the official board, nor to give prayers in church; they are not to take up collection, or be ordained with the same powers as their male counterparts. To the religious bigot, equal rights for women is patently the work of satan. Women who head other nations or otherwise do what men are "supposed to do," according to fundamentalist tradition, are considered the work of the devil.

Women are permitted to speak only "in tongues" during regular services. Whereas the dismisal prayer is occasionally given by a male member, women are never asked to pray in an intelligible language during a regular service. This may be one reason most messages "in tongues" are given by women. It's the only way they can be heard during the regular service. The irony is that in the very chapter of the Bible in which Paul discusses speaking "in tongues," he also says "it is a shame for a woman to speak in church." (See: 1 Cor. 14) This failure to follow biblical directive does not seem to disturb the fundamentalists, who claim to follow the Bible to the letter. The Bible directs women to dress with "shamefacedness and sobriety," and not with "gold, or pearls, or costly array." They are told their husbands are "the glory of God" while they are "the glory of the man." (It's not hard to tell the Bible was written by men.) Just so there is no confusion on the point, the Bible states that women are to be in subjection to men and tells the woman not to teach or to exercise authority over men.

With such unequivocal support from the biblical teachings of Paul and Peter, it is not difficult to understand the fundamentalist's attitude toward women. At the same time for the independent thinker, using John Adams' "free inquiry" approach to the Bible, these Bible teachings may well be unjust and not in keeping with the spirit of Christianity. The Founding Fathers were not reluctant to point out the fact that much in the Bible is "sublime," but not all of it. Jefferson said that often finding the good is like hunting for "diamonds in a dunghill." Mixing the free inquiry philosophy of Adams' with this Jefferson metaphor, it can be fairly concluded that on the subject of equal rights for women, the diamonds are on the ladies, and not in the Word.

Education

Much of the failure of the fundamentalist church to interpret the Bible in the light of modern knowledge lies in the lack of education of its clergy. A knowledge of the Bible is all that's required to go on TV, pointer in hand, and lecture from charts and illustrations on scientific and historic subjects. It is appalling to see TV evangelists with only a few years of grammar school as an educational background plus possibly some Bible college diploma, lecturing to millions. Some of these "educators" are even called "doctor" indicating a sheepskin - very appropriate - from some Bible college has been received. You would think they would be ashamed to teach with no adequate graduate training in the subjects on which they pontificate. But, lo, have no misgivings. They are not embarrassed. They have read the Book which to them contains the answers to all problems. In addition, they have been "called of God" and have special spiritual insights that transcend historic and scientific evidence which might conflict with the Bible or their personal revelations from on high. Remember, too, these preachers know their denomination's dogmas, and it would be dangerous to stray from the given line. Many a preacher has been defrocked after being found guilty of thinking without a license. So don't disturb these preachers with facts. In truth what John Adams called the "vanity of the human heart" has too great a share in determining such self-proclaimed anointed ones in their opinions on any subject.

Their lack of training would not be so bad if they did as Washington, and sought to educate themselves. But these are one-bookers. For them the Bible contains all the answers to all questions. Then if you are convinced the Bible holds all the wisdom one will ever need, then you and I too would proably lecture at will on any subject without chagrin.

The average small church fundamentalist preacher, poorly educated, but surrounded by parishioners who feel he is their earthly contact with God, is understandably not wanting to get too far afield in his theological thinking. It might muddy the waters and cause him to lose a good thing. In what other line of work could he wear expensive suits, keep his hands clean, have one or more luxury cars, live rent-free in a comfortable home paid for by others. Yes, it pays to be good. These pray for pay men - keep the women out, too much competition - find free trips, appearances on TV, and all that entertainment, plus a hall to lecture in to their heart's content, just too much to jeopardize with unorthodoxy and reason.

Censorship

To watch a charismatic preacher prance and stomp you would certainly think he had much in common with rock stars of the day; but rock music is another item on their list of things demonic. It seems someone decided to fix a rock record so that if you played it backwards and listened carefully you might be able to hear something resembling the word "satan." That did it! From that critical moment in the history of the fundamentalist church, rockers and rock music have been off limits, unless the words have a "Christian theme." Intrinsic musical quality of a particular piece of music is, of course, never involved in these judgments.

The quintessence of a successful devil-beating get together consist of having a standing room only crowd; and, as the main attraction, a repentant rock and roller. His testimony as to the evils of rock music will turn the crowd on by confirming their opinions of this modern sound along with their feelings of self-righteousness.

Had any good bonfires lately? Just wait till you are the first on your block to burn rock records! If you could have a performance like the one just described followed by a rock record burning, just think of the crowd you could raise. Think of the collection, and to top it all somebody might be "saved." To insure success you might consider a porn burn at the same time. Bring those dirty books and magazines. Pitch in, first thing you know you will have old satan on the run.

You will, of course, want to gain publicity for your event by getting the community into the act. Have a committee scan the shelves of the school library for books with racy themes. Don't forget to appoint another committee to picket the local mom and pop convenience store because they carry one or more girlie magazines. This should insure at least newspaper coverage.

Yes, since the Judeo-Christian religion is obsessed with circumcision and virginity, all sexy writings should certainly be consigned to the flames along with those rock records. Oops, I was about to forget those books on evolution. Get those too. Glory how they burn!

But wait. Are certain kinds of music and sex sinful? Since neither Jesus nor the devil left any writings, we will just have to take the word of those who claim to know their opinions on these subjects. What better authority than your local fundamentalist church?

Now hold on here another minute, weren't these same churches against American jazz at its inception? Could it have been because it was conceived in the brothels of New Orleans and the speakeasys of Chicago? Is jazz not now generally considered our nation's only true native art form? A problem now arises. Just suppose the local purifier of our thoughts, viewing, and listening habits, discovers that Mozart had pre-marital sex. Hold on tight to those classical records, they might be next on the wax-to-burn hit parade. And suppose - just suppose - somebody had the temerity to point out to them the erotica in the Bible. What, you mean you haven't read the Song of Solomon? For shame! Can't you just imagine how all this mind purging would set with the Founding Fathers? Let us pray.

The Bible

All this may seem far afield from the life of Jesus which so concerned the Founding Fathers, particularly Jefferson. Ostensibly, today's religious fanatics are in business to promote Bible-based Christianity. It then behooves us to take a look at the Word.

When stripped of its patina of supposed Deitistic endorsement, reason suggests that the writers of the Bible were just plain people. No claim is made within its covers that any of its authors were divine. Interestingly, some of its stories emphasize this point. Cornelius tried to worship the man we now call "Saint Peter" whose reaction was: "Stand up, I myself also am a man." "Saint Paul" said essentially the same thing to the people of Lystra when they tried to treat him as a god. Yet Peter and Paul, whose combined writings make up over half of the New Testament, are quoted from pulpits as if these men were what they said they were not, i.e. gods.

In fact all the books of the Bible were written by men. It was not lowered from heaven on a string; but written by many perfectly ordinary men whose powers of memory and observation varied. There is no statement in the Bible that Paul ever saw

Jesus in the flesh. It is also true that not one single word of either the New or the Old Testament has been found in its original manuscript. What we have are copies of copies of the books of the Bible. During a period of more than two thousand years, until the printing press was developed, each succeeding rendition of these writings was laboriously copied by hand, usually by an adoring scribe whose desire to harmonize and embellish the text must have been compelling.

As we have seen, no one admired the philosophy of Jesus more than Jefferson; yet he, and others among the Founding Fathers, realized the true nature of the Bible, both its strengths and weaknesses.

The principal dogma of the fundamentalist is that the Bible is the inerrant, infallible Word of God containing no contradictions. Yet among those who founded our nation were several dissenters from this dogma. They knew the Bible was a rich storehouse of stories and philosophy. They also felt that to believe all its stories was to confuse fact with fiction, history with lyric poetry.

A careful study of the Bible reveals contradictions, and errors too numerous to go into here. Such studies have been made not only by some of the Founding Fathers; but, by many in search of the historic Jesus, including this author.[127] It should appeal to reason that were the Old Testament complete and sufficient, there would be no need for a New Testament. For example, in the Book of Leviticus paragraph after paragraph in chapter eleven details the creatures that are not to be eaten. In the New Testament, God tells Peter that "all manner of four footed beasts, and creeping things, and fowls of the air" may be eaten (Acts 10:9-16).

The fundamentalists are caught in an embarassing situation. Their dogma that the Bible is infallible and inerrant, containing the answers to all of mankinds problems, is patently false. Their own actions, of course, belie such professed belief. When they are struck with illness, they both read their Bible and seek medical care. This well illustrates the fact that pragmatically man's existence has two components: the physical and the spiritual.

[127] Jack Lasley, **The Power Within** (NISGO Publications, 1984).

The fundamentalist gets into difficulty when he confuses the two. They cite Isaiah 53:5 "with his stripes we are healed" and claim that healing was provided in the Atonement. They preach it is not God's will that any believer be sick. Since believers and non-believers get sick and die in about equal proportion, these fundamentalists have either misunderstood the Bible or God has lost control.

The Bible is an anthology of stories, fables, philosophy, and poetry. Only in the sense that all things come from God can it be said that the Bible is the word of God. Even the fundamentalists do not contend that the Bible was written by the hand of God, but by men inspired by the Spirit of God working in them. This is exactly the point we wish to make, i.e. men have said that other men have written the words of God. Repeated often enough and solemnized by ecclesiastical councils, the idea that the Bible somehow was divinely authored becomes accepted without question, except by those of reasoning minds. In truth the dogma was created by what Jefferson calls "priestcraft." In writing to his nephew he reminded the lad that religion is too important a matter not to investigate thoroughly. Jefferson's own investigations proved to him that there is much in the Bible that lacks truth and inspiration.

It should be noted, too, that some of the Bible's chief luminaries, including some of its principal authors, failed to lead exemplary lives. Moses is credited with writing the first five books of the Old Testament; David most of the Psalms; and, Paul is believed to have authored over half of the New Testament. Each was involved in murder and lesser transgressions. So, when we sit in reverential silence Sunday mornings listening to what they wrote, we might just remember the true source of the words we hear. If we believe we are hearing the Word of God from a man of God, we might be wrong on both counts.

An objective reading of the Bible and its history is threatening to the fundamentalist. Mull through its pages. See if you can find a good piece against slavery or racial prejudice. Are you happy with the Bible's handling of the matter of equal rights for women? Do you feel the treatment for leprosy outlined in chapters 13 and 14 of Leviticus represents the medical treatment you would wish to receive if you were infected with that disease?

Manifestly, the Bible contains many beautifully expressive passages and well-told stories. But to use it to prove historic or scientific facts, or as a foretelling of our destiny, is subject to reasonable questioning considering the source of these writings. Should we, just to illustrate the point, consider it holy writ that the "elements shall melt with fervent heat, the earth also and the works that are therein shall be burned up" (2 Pet. 3:10). That is what Peter wrote. Shall we sit idly by as blood runs to the horse's bridles at the battle of Armageddon (See: chapters 14, 15 and 16 of Revelation)? Because of these and other statements in the Bible, fundamentalists apparently feel a nuclear holocaust is inevitable, even welcome if it will usher in the return of Jesus. What blasphemies they entertain in the name of piety! It could be argued that a just God would not preordain the destruction of the earth and its people; thus to refrain from the use of law, order, and world government to prevent nuclear disaster, because of the writings of men who lived hundreds of years ago, is not according to holy writ but is nonsense in the extreme.

If we grant for the sake of argument that all those who wrote the Bible were inspired by God, does it make sense to also say that no other men have been so inspired? By what authority shall we exclude Mohammed and others who claimed to have received messages from God? Shall we prove the exclusiveness of the Bible by quoting the Bible?

Let us then think for ourselves, using our God-given reason which is our best shield against those who would use the Bible for selfish gain. Commenting on how the spirit of Jesus has been corrupted by priestcraft, Jefferson wrote: ". . . before his principles were departed from by those who professed to be his special servants, and perverted into an engine for enslaving mankind, and aggrandizing their oppressors . . . the purest system of morals ever before preached to man has been adulterated and sophisticated by artificial constructions, into a mere contrivance to filch wealth and power to themselves . . . ." Still we can be encouraged by the prediction of John Adams that the genuine doctrines of Jesus, "so long perverted by his pseudopriests, will again be restored to their original purity" and that "this reformation will advance with the other improvements of the human mind."

Love God?

We are commanded by Jesus to love God with all of our heart, soul, and mind (Mat. 22: 36-37). From Samuel Adams to Thomas Paine we cover the spectrum of various religious beliefs of the Christians and Deists that brought our nation into being. As with Job of the Old Testament, they all seemed to have respected the awesome power of the force that rules the universe. But unlike the charismatic fundamentalists, they were not of the "honk if you love Jesus," fawning, obsequious bent. We read earlier of Jefferson's observations regarding a Richmond, Virginia church in which he objected to "meetings and praying parties" where the participants poured forth "the effusions of their love of Jesus, in terms as amatory and carnal, as their modesty would permit them to use to a mere earthly lover." He also objected to what he called the fear in religion "under which weak minds are serviley crouched."

As the Christian passes through this life he watches his own body deteriorate and life about him recycled into new forms of matter. He takes solice in the biblical promise that there is a spirit world in the hereafter where all will be righted and justice and mercy will be the rule. In this Christian heaven there will be no more sorrow, pain, and suffering. To paraphrase the old hymn, after one has been there ten thousand years, it will all have just begun.

Still, if this life is any indication of the measure of justice and mercy we are to receive in heaven, we have cause for concern. Our celebrations on earth of the love of God may not only be premature but overdone if we rely on empirical evidence only.

Paine was offended by talk of God as a destroyer and unjust judge. Probably most of the other Found-in Fathers would be similarly put off by such a portrayal of the Deity. But using the "reason" that Paine so admired, let us consider the evidence.

What force or power is accountable for the natural disasters that cause us such distress? Shall we put the blame on the devil and thereby create another god to join the Trinity? If we do, we sink ever deeper into the multi-god, Hellenistic, quagmire Jefferson warned against. Let us continue our investigation of the empirical evidence.

If you could be God, would you:

1. Create the devil?
2. Kill everyone on earth except eight persons?
3. Plan and carry out the death of Jesus?
4. Create all the germs, viruses, and other agents that have plagued all creatures since life began?
5. Allow babies to be born with deformities?
6. Permit entire open cities to be destroyed by nuclear bombardment?
7. Cause the sins of the fathers to be visited on the sons to the third and fourth generation?
8. Plan a war (Armageddon) in which blood will flow to the horses bridles?
9. Destroy the earth and its elements by fire?

This is the God of the fundamentalist. For the theologian, moralist, sociologist, ecologist, all those engaged in life sciences, ethics, and for Christians generally, these Bible based attributes of God are difficult to avoid.

Our efforts on earth are deemed "good" when we perform useful, constructive work, and do what we can to ease suffering, and prevent death and destruction. We even extend these efforts to animals. Beached whales are taken to marine biological facilities. Creatures of all kinds are taken to shelters and sanctuaries when found sick or wounded. It is our nature to fight nature and not let it run its course. We create endangered species lists and consider heroes those who find vaccines and other means to destroy the deforming and deadly agents of nature that threaten man and beast. Nature is truly bloody in tooth and claw. Nothing walks, crawls, or swims that does not have myriads of such agents set to attack its body. Those who wrote the Bible thought of them as evil spirits sent by satan. We know them to be a material part of the structure that has been with us since early in the Creation process. The advent of the microscope and the advance of science have given us new insights into the previously unseen, microscopic world of genes, genetic constructions, germs, and viruses. The latest serums and medical techniques have replaced the mud and spittle of Bible days.

There are indeed those times when we are so threatened by infirmities that we turn in our desperation to those who can give us spiritual solace. At such times our reason is so encumbered with anxiety that we are far from being free agents, or objective thinkers. When a person feels death clutching at his vitals, in his stricken condition he naturally turns to any that might ameliorate - if not cure - his condition. It's the Errol Flynn syndrome. It is said that the late actor during his last illness was asked what turned him toward seeking spiritual help. His classic reply was: "What have I got to lose?"

It can certainly do no harm to seek a boon from the Maker of heaven and earth by the nearest available route. Obviously such petitions are not always granted. However, even if such a beneficent dispensation is forthcoming, it patently does not arrest the injustices in the system borne by others. The engines of pain and despair are endemic and profuse, and it does not lessen these inequities if the Maker relieves only a few of them. What of those who daily suffer unjustly and go to their graves without compensatory relief? To trot out the biblical story of Adam and Eve to justify these inequities, does little to support the good-God hypothesis.

It is in times when our emotions are unfettered; when our minds are clearest and most objective, that we can conclude there is much injustice built into the universe - when viewed with a reasoned perspective. If we abandon this keystone of our rational thought and moral code, we begin to construct a double standard: One for people, and another for God. Soon we begin to justify all manner of human calamities, accidents, and disorders in general, on the basis that God knows best. The child born deformed, or who dies from one of the multitude of microscopic organisms injected into the world, has clearly not been protected by an "all-good" God. Still this concept of an all-good God is basic to fundamentalism. If there is a good God, surely It would admire that believer who is honest in his emotional relationships; one who is not hypocritical in his feelings toward mankind and God. From Abraham to Jesus and including Moses, the men of the Bible were usually honest with God. When they objected to what was going on, they said so. Yet today's effusive in-church statements of love for God are never supplemented with sincere objections to the unjust way many just people suffer because of the very nature of Creation. Such statements would be considered shocking, even blasphemous.

The hypocrisy Jesus so vehemently opposed is alive and well in the churches of the land. It is time we became honest with God. Praise him for the good things, and let him know when we feel injustice has been, or is being done regardless of its source. Fakery before God fools no one but ourselves. If there is an all-good God, the empirical evidence shows there cannot be an all-powerful God, as the inequities of this life are simply too great and numerous to support the validity of such a dual hypothesis.

Is God Good?
We tend to define what is "good" on the basis of human interrelatednesses and feelings, judging all happenings on the basis of the Bentham pleasure/pain calculus. Getting outside this human-oriented perspective may be difficult, but

it can bring a new and important quotient into our conception of "goodness." By being all-encompassing in our definition, we extend our view beyond human feelings to bring in the entire universe. Now "good" takes on new meaning. It becomes that which contributes to the regeneration and on-going of the universe . . . that which makes it tick, as it were.

John Adams touched on this. Let us again recall what he wrote: "The Creator looked into the remotest futurity, and saw his great designs accomplished by this inextricable, this mysterious complication of causes. But to rise still higher, this solar system is but one very small wheel in the great, the astonishing machine of the world. Those stars, that twinkle in the heavens, have each of them a choir of planets, comets, and satellites, dancing round them, playing mutually on each other, and all, together, playing on the other systems that lie around them.

"Our system, considered as one body hanging on its center of gravity, may affect and be affected by all the other systems within the compass of creation. Thus it is highly probable every particle of matter influences and is influenced by every other particle in the whole collected universe."

Thus there is no way a created being can escape playing out its role in the universal plan. No particular species fares any better than any other. Each has its life cycle and role to play. Each its own joys and terrors. No evidence supports the claim that man's existence in the overall spread of life on earth is in any special position as to equity, justice and mercy vis-a-vis the creation. We are not rewarded for goodness and punished for evil-doing; and, even though we seek to impose this standard on our existence, it is not the natural way the system operates.

Each creature, no matter how it acts in this life, inescapably contributes to the smooth functioning of the whole system. It is this interrelatedness - this service, if you will - to the entire creation that may win for each an equal position in the hereafter. Since ostensibly this "service" complies with the intent of the Creator, each life should share equally with its own kind in heaven.

In this context, what individual creatures do during their lives and the length of their lives and experiences they encounter may be, in varying degrees, important to them and others, but makes no difference in the continuation of the integrated whole. It is not that the individual creature makes no difference, it is that what it does is unimportant to this eternal enterprise and oneness. An individual life may be good, or bad by our social standards; it may end early or reach extended years; it may reproduce its kind or not; its species may become extinct, and worlds may crumble, but others will take their places. Matter is being recycled in the eternal process of renewal which remains as inviolable as it has been since the creation.

Thus unavoidably the role of the individual creature is played out as a temporary repository for atomic materials. At the death of the individual, this matter is liberated to find its way again into another combination of particles in the vast storehouse of matter that continues to act and react, assemble and disassemble. Only the WHOLE is perfect. We unwittingly serve this whole integrated perfection by our very existence. Therefore, all participants in this material perfection serve it, and since their actions do not jeopardize its functioning no matter what they do, they are then "good" and serve the Maker of the system of perfection as a part thereof. Thus viewed, the Author of the universe can be seen as the Creator of a perfectly functioning universal machine of which all creatures are a salutary part.

The time we spend in directing others in what they should do - as if their eternal existence depended on what we deem to be good among men - may be misdirected energy, and have no bearing on their eternal existence. It could well be that goodness of this kind interests the Creator not one iota. Goodness in the universal sense is insured and is inviolable ab initio. The spiritual, everlasting reward of all creatures may not be dependent on what Jefferson called the "formulations of men," but guaranteed by the Creator to all Its creatures because they have played their part in the organized, integrated, ongoing whole of creation. No creature would be swept into eternal flames because of inherent weakness. The fundamentalist's dogma that the great preponderance of people will not be "saved," but will burn in everlasting hell does little to enhance the "good-God" doctrine. After all, no one asked to be created. We are imperfect products by design of the Creator, involuntarily here, proceeding through the perfectly functioning creation. So viewed God has not lost control, but is supremely in command. Pain and suffering become non-entities from the standpoint of this universal "goodness."

But in this analysis, we have strayed far afield from the ordinary concepts of right and wrong, good and bad, and have developed, like St. Paul and other religionists, a man-made, rhetorical formulation, designed to convince our minds that God is good. Unlike fundamentalist dogma, it has the advantage of seeing all people not as depraved, but as eminently worthy sons and daughters of God, bound for heaven, no matter what form of mischief their uniqueness, individualism, and imperfections get them into.

We may then conclude, as did Job of old, that God is fearsome, full of wonders, and awe inspiring, but these are not synonyms or euphemisms for goodness. Only in a highly structured sense, and within an hypothesis that omits most of the usual human norms of good and evil, can God be said to be "good."

Bigotry

During the '60's much attention was directed - and rightly so - toward racial bigots in our midst. Mostly decried were those who would deny equal rights to blacks. We have always had those who were prejudiced against blacks, whites, Jews, Catholics, women, and so on. But today's so-called full gospel, evangelical, fundamentalist is in a league apart. Behind their amicable facade often hides a bigotry that far surpasses that of racial or creedal hatreds. Hidden amid their acknowledged good qualities is a doctrine that says that all who are not "saved" - according to their definition of that term - will, on their death, not go to heaven, but spend eternity in hell. Those they deem unworthy to be with God in the hereafter include Protestants who - in their terms - have not fully "accepted Jesus as their personal savior." According to some, a believer should also have "been filled with the Holy Ghost with evidence of speaking in tongues." Of course this excludes not only most Americans but most of the people on earth. Remember the first duty of the fundamentalist is to obey the Great Commission of Jesus to take the gospel to all the world. This directive overrides all other earthly obligations.

Since the advent of TV and the rise of the shout and stomp, entertainment-oriented evangelist as a political phenomenon, a serious problem has arisen which deserves the careful consideration of the entire nation. Suppose, for example, we were to elect one of these religious bigots as President of the United States. Whom would he appoint to his cabinet or nominate for the Supreme Court? Would not ambassadors be selected with an eye toward carrying out the Great Commission abroad? Clearly those who were "unsaved" would not qualify. Among such non-qualifiers would be Jews, Muslims and most professing Christians. Lest we forget, God will deny entry into heaven to the "unsaved" and they will spend eternity in hell; so clearly no God fearing fundamentalists would appoint such a person to public office. Thus the list of potential appointees would soon dwindle down to a precious few. Can you imagine a Supreme Court packed with TV evangelists? Heaven forbid!

This potential for ineptness in high places is not as far fetched as it might have been in the past. The juxtaposition of the advent of TV and a desire at all cost to get back to basic standards has sent us scurrying off to find these lost values among the most bigoted group the nation has ever spawned. Pluralism is a key factor in the greatness of America. We have made great strides in our attempt to rid our nation of the prejudices that may have denied Al Smith and Adlai Stevenson the Presidency, and today impedes women and certain minorities in their efforts to attain public office. Such prejudices should not be allowed to keep fundamentalists from public office if they can lay aside their fundamentalism for the good of the country. Yet the views of the radical right - which we are concerned with here - are so bizarre, their commitment against personal freedom so deep seated, that the electorate can ignore them only at its peril. To illustrate, under fundamentalist doctrine it is considered high sin to change one world of The Word. Since Benjamin Franklin edited the Lord's Prayer and Thomas Jefferson re-wrote the New Testament, these Founding Fathers would not be considered fit to hold public office under a radical fundamentalist regime (see: Rev. 22:19; Ex. 32:33; Ps. 69:28). And can you imagine fundamentalist support for John Adams or Thomas Paine?

The political campaigns of the religious right would probably be run under the guise of restoring America's lost values. Sounds good, and would certainly have wide voter appeal. But before you cast your ballot for their candidates, find out what they mean by such terms as "like precious faith" and "the brethren." You may be voting for a bigoted, censorship minded, freedom destroying, military minded, elite group that could turn our nation from a democracy into a theocracy overnight. It has happened elsewhere, it must not happen here. By the way, have you seen one of their youth corps arrayed in quasi-military uniforms marching down the aisles of your local fundamentalist church? Believe me, you don't want to.

The quick-draw attitude that has gotten our nation into such difficulties abroad, is right in line with fundamentalist philosophy. Their attitude towards violence keeps them from touching the Sermon on the Mount except lightly and in passing. Whipping children, support for capital punishment, militarism, and the denial of women's rights and basic human equality, are all accepted and encouraged. It would not only be ironic but tragic if we should lose our freedoms to radical religious conservatives who claim to be the bearers of God's will for our nation and its future.

THE

WAY

IT

WILL

BE

The Great Republic Of Humanity

With the development of nuclear armaments and their intercontinental delivery systems, the earth's people had every right to expect protection by their governments. But national governments seem bent on equating one-upsmanship in weapons of destruction with security. How secure can one feel with atomic megatonage hanging over his head, knowing full well that its control rests in a balance of terror, treaties, and summit conferences? Where is the faith in protection through law and government shared by the Founding Fathers?

What has this to do with religion? Just this. If there is a God of mercy, justice and love, It can surely not be happy with so terrifying and fragile a world system as now exists; one that threatens our very species. If we had the revolutionary spirit of those we revere as patriots, we would bring law and government to bear on the problems of world security and human rights. Yet, we deem such advocates radicals, left wingers, one-worlders, Communists, subversive, and so on. Interestingly, the Bible does not discourage world government per se. It does warn against the enthronement of a great deceiver, a "beast," and Antichrist who will sit in the temple of God. The inference is that this worshipped being is to be a theocratic monster. Unfortunately, these passages have been used by some fundamentalists as a warning against the rise of Catholicism and Muslimism.

The Bible goes on to predict a time when Jesus will rule the earth. If we interpret this to mean the world rule of love - since God is love - we have biblical endorsement of just world government whereby mankind can be spared the hatreds and violence that accompanies international warfare, but this is certainly not the fundamentalist view.

The major force in opposition to a world under law, is the so-called full gospel, evangelical fundamentalists. They feel that the Bible speaks of Armageddon and thus it must be. And what better time than now, they reason, to let the blood run "even unto the horse bridles, by the space of a thousand and six hundred furlongs," because this event would precede and presage the earthly reign of Jesus Christ! So there is the problem of the two r's - radical religionists - who await the burning of the world as God ordained writ, and see "one world government" as involving the enthronement of the Antichrist. Some even call the large NATO computer in the Netherlands as the Beast of Belgium," a reference to the "beast" of Revelation.

The so-called full gospel Christians picture themselves as the embodiment of exemplary patriotism. Attend one of their services around the Fourth of July and watch their idolatry as they unfurl Old Glory and pledge allegiance in the temple of the Lord to the . . . United States! God and Jesus being temporarily shelved.

Of course they feel the United Nations is a Communist plot. No thought is given to raising the effectiveness of the UN as a vital force in man's progress toward a better world. Lost is the spirit of San Francisco when, at its birth, the world saw the UN as the way to universal survival in freedom. This dream has been lost to fear. We have been paralyzed by thoughts of surrendering sovereignty, and fear of Communism, socialism, and xenophobia generally, pressed on us by the radical right.

But the Pentagon is not the symbol we celebrate on the Fourth of July. Rather, it is the Statue of Liberty that stands for the best that is in us. We traditionally care for the plight of all humans, not just those of one religion or form of government. It is in this tradition that we should proceed toward finding a solution to the nuclear balance of terror.

If we had the political imagination and ingenuity of our nation's Founding Fathers - whom we celebrate with such gusto as patriots - we would ourselves become revolutionaries against the system of modern nation-states that seek to control man's destiny by threats of nuclear extinction; we would substitute law and popular government of the whole for this life-threatening caotic balance of terror.

The elevation of law and government to the international level of human endeavor should be our quest. The spirit of July 4, 1776, might then be re-kindled for an even wider and nobler purpose: that of truly saving mankind through a governed world.

To be effective, the movement for a peaceful world must involve the people of all nations. It must not only be world-wide, but encompass more than disarmament and peace advocacy. There must be the positiveness of at least the outline of a plan. Being against war is not enough to get the job done. What, say the skeptics, about the shoebox bomb, the terrorist; what of those who would use disarmament as a ploy to gain control of those weapons remaining after general disarmament. Scary, what? But does not law and order under just government hold a better prospect for the future than a continuation down the dead end street toward nuclear disaster?

Consider the madness now that passes for security. Bombs are secreted in the earth and under the seas with enough power to kill every human many times over. In the face of this threat, we have no plan for containment. What we do have is summitry wherein bargains are struck for meaningless reductions in the number of missiles. What does it matter if our species can be extinguished 60 times over rather than 100. Dead is dead, as much one way as the other. All the while the business of war preparation continues while the art of peace is reduced to summit conferences and spy exchanges.

Needed is a government by and for all people ,under which the people can supervise the destruction of armaments down to the level needed to keep the peace. This is the way law and order proceeds in our cities and between the states of both the United States and Russia. For example, Carolinians do not arm to protect themselves from Virginians; nor do the people of the Ukraine arm to prevent an incursion by Georgians. Why the world's largest super powers are bent on burying the human race is beyond understanding. Until the people speak truth to the world's powers, mutual intimidation will continue until one nation, by accident or design, launches the first missile. Should that occur, colored

150 /

telephones are all that stand in the way of our mutual destruction. There is no strong, overarching authority in existence to prevent a subsequent holocaust, and to supervise the elimination of these weapons.

The Founding Fathers of our nation were faced with the task of bringing together states containing a wide variety of people from the back bay Bostonian to the backwoodsmen of Virgina and the Carolinas. These divergent states and their people were to be brought together to achieve stated objectives dealing with their freedom and security. These should be our objectives today for all the peoples of the earth. Yet we plan their destruction! As with the Founding Fathers, our faith should lie with the people and their ability to form a democratic government of the whole to secure for all the blessings of freedom and security.

The Founding Fathers went at their task influenced, but not controlled, by movements and governments of the past. They stood up to the British Empire, and became revolutionaries in the cause of liberty. The Peace Movement must say to the powers of the world, "we the people will no longer be held hostage to a balance of terror that threatens our species."

While an end to international violence may be visionary, as was the dream of an end to racial discrimination, such a goal can form the basis of a far better world wherein violence is contained, if not eliminated. The aim of such a movement would be to seek a world arrangement of nations wherein the people, not the major power leaders, have control of the destiny of mankind. This means democratic world government able to minimize the threat or use of any weapons that threaten our species. Then, should a weapon be launched, the act would not result in a blinding exchange of missiles. Rather, the threat to world peace would be felt by all people in a perspective of the oneness we feel today toward our family, town, state, and nation. Herein we have the seeds of true brotherly love advocated by Jesus in the Sermon on the Mount and so blatantly distorted by Christian fanatics.

The peace movement must also say in effect:
"Certainly we are against war and, in addition,
we are for democratic world government as the
best way to achieve freedom from the threat of
annihilation." This means we must speak up to those
in power throughout the world. They must be shaken.
Their present reluctance to proceed with the law
and order way to peace stems from fear and
entrenched self-interest.

This is a call for the common sense way to save
the species. It is a call for democratic international
government. By the use of world-wide
demonstrations, demand should be made that there
be held a Constitutional Convention to draw a
people's constitutional document that includes a
Bill of Rights of the People. The option is simple;
we can do it now or after the Third World War,
assuming for the sake of this postulate that someone
remains.

It was Franklin Roosevelt who said that fear
could stifle this nation, and so it has. Stifled us
from taking the steps consistent with our past to
rid the world of the scourge of nuclear holocaust,
while at the same time insuring maximum freedoms
for all people. What an accolade we toss the communists when we consider peace a communist plot.

If adjustments to our life style are involved in
the transition to world government, what a small
price to pay for what we will gain. We are not
so committed to the status quo that we must commit
suicide to preserve it. That sounds like our attitude
toward My Lai in Vietnam, when we decided to
destroy the town in order to "save" it.

Those of us who marched with Martin Luther
King in the 60's, and were later gassed and jailed
in the May Day demonstrations of the early 70's
against the Vietnam war, were both idealistic and
pragmatic. Ideally we wished for an end to all
bigotry and war. Practically we realized we might
be able to accomplish the dual purpose of improving
the lot of blacks in this country and ending the
war in Vietnam. It would be foolish for anyone
to deny the accomplishment of both ends by these

uprisings of our nation's citizens. It was the people, not the nation's elected officials, that showed the way the country must go to be consistent with its heritage. So many of our present difficulties stem not from those who opposed that war, but from those leaders who pursued it.

Today we may be turned off by revolutionaries; yet, we best not lose sight of the fact that our own patriots were rebels in the cause of human freedom. Samuel Adams used Lord North's Tea Act as a springboard for the Boston Tea Party and the assembling of the Continental Congress. Many of the Founding Fathers demonstrated their feelings to their government in England. We must do the same to our respective national governments in the cause of world government. Much as the Founding Fathers brought our nation first into confederation then into government of the whole, the world has had its League of Nations and United Nations. The time is past due for an international government of the whole.

We lost the golden opportunity after World War II to make the United Nations into a world government. What we did in forming the UN was clearly aimed in the direction of creating a world authority to care for the needs of people everywhere. But, as time passed and the memory of that war dimmed, we were overtaken by the negativisms of communism, and lost sight of the greater challenge of creating an international organization sufficiently strong to insure peace with freedom. In this regard, read again what Jefferson had to say about the attitude of the people following the war of independence: "It can never be too often repeated, that the time for fixing every essential right on a legal basis is while our rulers are honest, and ourselves united. From the conclusion of this war we shall be going down hill. It will not then be necessary to resort every moment to the people for support. They will be forgotten, therefore, and their rights disregarded. They will forget themselves, but in the sole faculty of making money, and will never think of uniting to effect a due respect for their rights. The shackles, therefore, which shall not be knocked off at the conclusion of this war, will remain on us long, will be made heavier and heavier till our rights shall revive or expire in a convulsion." [128]

Will our failure to strengthen the United Nations since the close of World War II mean that we will expire in a convulsion of nuclear missiles? Not if we join with the people of goodwill in all nations to begin the quest for a governed world.

In a letter to Lafayette, George Washington wrote he considered himself a "citizen of that great republic of humanity," and envisioned a time when there would be an end of the "devastations and horrors of war." [129] May we consider ourselves as citizens of that same republic as we proceed, undeterred by religious fanaticism, toward liberty and justice for all. Let us begin this noblest of quests in the spirit of Thomas Paine, who wrote: "The world is my country, all mankind are my brethren . . . ." [130]

[128] Supra, pp. 12-13.
[129] Supra, pp. 54-55.
[130] Supra, p. 28.